To Tony and ~~
with whom I love sha~~
To Sue for her ongoing ~~
throughout the years.

And to Christopher Miller,
who inspired me to take the first step.

More at: www.dialanikolaeva.com
www.perfectpresentshop.co.uk

Index

Introduction	4
Northern Europe	5
Denmark I Know What I Have Learned	6
Frikadelle	7
Estonia The Devil's Wedding	8
Mulgipuder Mulgi kapsad	9
Finland The Birth of Wainamoinen	10
Lohikeitto	11
Iceland The Merman	12
Skyr with Berries	13
Ireland The Salmon of Knowledge	14
Colcannon	15
Latvia The White Deer	16
Grey Peas with Bacon	17
Lithuania The Swan Queen	18
Cold Beet Soup	19
Norway The Giant Who Had No Heart in His Body	20
Fiskekaker	21
Sweden The Lady of Pintorp	22
Semla	23
United Kingdom The Marriage of Robin and Blue Tit	24
Welsh Rarebit	25
Central Europe	27
Austria Hansel and Gretel	28
Wiener Schnitzel	29
Switzerland The Story of William Tell	30
Rösti	31
Liechtenstein The White Horse of Lochgass	32
Käsknöpfle	33
Monaco Virtue and Fortune in Monte Carlo	34
Socca	35
Southern Europe	37
Albania For The Love of a Dove	38
Tavë Kosi	39
Andorra The Piper of Ordino	40
Escudella	41
Bosnia and Herzegovina The Dragon's Strength	42
Ćevapi	43
Croatia Ban Dragonja	44
Pašticada	45
Greece Clash of the Titans	46
Spanakopita	47
Italy The Merchant	48
Pasta al Pomodoro	49
Malta The Tale of the Fisherman's Son	50
Timpana	51
Montenegro The Legend of Black Lake	52
Kačamak	53
North Macedonia Justice Never Dies	54
Tavče Gravče	55
Portugal St. Anthony's Godchild	56
Pastéis de Nata	57
San Marino The Legend of Saint Peter's Mother	58
Torta Tre Monti	59

Index

Serbia How to Choose a Wife	60
Pileći Paprikaš	61
Slovenia The Tale Of Goldhorn	62
Potica	63
Spain The Legend of the Spider	64
Tortilla Española	65
Eastern Europe	67
Belarus The Mower and the Wolf	68
Draniki	69
Bulgaria The Witty Petar	70
Banitsa	71
Czech Republic The Long-Desired Child	72
Svickova	73
Hungary The Gold Bread	74
Goulash	75
Moldova The Pot of Gold	76
Mămăligă	77
Poland Twardowski	78
Pierogi	79
Romania The Enchanted Pig	80
Ciorbă de burtă	81
Russia Baba Yaga	82
Blini	83
Slovakia The Story of Three Wicked Yezinkas	84
Bryndzové Halušky	85
Ukraine How the Dog Found Himself a Master	86
Borscht	87
Western Europe	89
Belgium The Magic Cap	90
Stoofvlees	91
France The Wild Boar	92
Quiche Lorraine	93
Germany Ashenputtel	94
Sauerbraten	95
Luxembourg The Legend of Beautiful Melusina	96
Judd mat Gaardebounen	97
Netherlands The Mouldy Penny	98
Stamppot	99

For the full stories and more recipes
follow us at:
www.youtube.com/@DialasLittleKitchen

Introduction

Welcome to Taste-Tales, a journey through Europe for the Whole Family. A special cookbook that blends traditional recipes from every corner of Europe with captivating folk stories that will transport your family to faraway lands. This book is more than just a collection of meals—it's an opportunity for busy parents to engage with their children, share the joy of cooking, and inspire creativity through both food and storytelling.

My love for travel and food has always connected me to the people and cultures of different countries. And through this cookbook, I want to offer families a chance to travel without leaving their kitchen. Each recipe is paired with a folk tale, allowing your family to immerse themselves in the rich traditions of European countries, from the fairy-tale forests of Scandinavia to the sun-soaked coasts of the Mediterranean.

Cooking with children can be a fun, educational experience that fosters healthy eating habits, teaches new skills, and creates lasting memories. These recipes have been carefully selected to balance simplicity with tradition, making them suitable for busy weeknights or special occasions. Whether it's preparing hearty dinners or creating fun desserts, these meals are meant to be enjoyed together—by both young hands and experienced ones.

Each recipe in this book is structured to make the cooking process easier for busy parents, with clear steps, helpful tips, and a mix of vegan, vegetarian, and gluten-free options. The accompanying stories are short, engaging, and perfect for inspiring children while waiting for the meal to cook.

So gather your ingredients, gather your children, and let's embark on a journey through Europe, one meal at a time.

Northern Europe

I Know What I Have Learned

Denmark

Once upon a time, there was an old man with three daughters, each married to a troll who lived underground. One day, he decided to visit them, and his wife packed him some dry bread for the journey. When he got hungry, he sat down by a mound to eat, and suddenly, his youngest daughter popped out and invited him in. Her troll husband soon arrived, and when his wife asked him to get meat, he simply banged his head on a beam to get some! Amazed, the old man went home with a sack of gold as a gift.

On his way back, he left the sack of money to check on his cow, only to find it gone when he returned! A thief had taken it. His wife scolded him, but he just chuckled and said, "I learned something!"

Next, he visited his second daughter. Her troll husband made candles by lighting his own fingers! Once again, the old man received two sacks of money, but he left them by the roadside—and, once again, they were stolen. His wife grew even more upset, but he just laughed, saying he'd learned more things.

Finally, he visited his oldest daughter. This time, her troll husband caught fish by jumping into the lake. The man got three sacks of gold this time but left them behind, thinking his wooden shoes would guard them. Of course, a thief took them, too!

Back home, the man tried to copy the trolls' tricks. He banged his head for meat, burned his fingers for light, and even jumped in a lake to catch fish—but nothing worked! He ended up wet, bruised, and hungry, but he just laughed, saying, "Well, at least I had a grand adventure!"

Frikadelle (Meatballs)

Serves: 4

Introduction:
Frikadelle are Danish meatballs traditionally served with potatoes and gravy. This hearty meal is a beloved family favourite in Denmark and can be prepared quickly.

Ingredients:
500g minced pork
1 small onion, finely chopped
1 egg
2 tbsp breadcrumbs
Salt and pepper to taste
Butter or oil for frying

Instructions:
1. Mix the minced pork, chopped onion, egg, breadcrumbs, salt, and pepper in a large bowl.
2. Shape the mixture into small meatballs with your hands.
3. Heat the butter or oil in a frying pan over medium heat and cook the meatballs until browned and cooked through, about 10 minutes.
4. Serve with mashed potatoes and gravy.

Tips/Substitutions:
For a healthier version, substitute half of the pork with ground turkey or chicken.
For a gluten-free option, use gluten-free breadcrumbs.
Serve with a side of roasted vegetables for extra nutrition.

Time to Prep/Cook:
Prep time: 10 minutes
Cook time: 15 minutes

The Devil's Wedding

Estonia

Long ago, a poor peasant named Ants lived in a small village. One day, while collecting firewood in the forest, he stumbled upon a strange sight—a group of demons preparing for a wedding! Curious, he hid nearby, watching the eerie scene. Suddenly, the devil himself spotted Ants and invited him to join the celebration. At first, Ants hesitated, but the devil promised a great reward, so he agreed.

Ants was taken to the wedding feast, filled with strange creatures, magical music, and delicious food. But soon, Ants noticed something shocking: the bride was a young woman from his village who had gone missing! Furious, he demanded that the devil let her go.

The devil laughed and refused, challenging Ants to a game of cards. If Ants won, the young woman would be freed; if he lost, she'd stay. Ants was skilled at cards, but he knew he needed extra help for this game. He secretly prayed for God's guidance.

The game began, and Ants found himself winning hand after hand, thanks to divine help. The devil, furious, tried to cheat, but Ants caught him every time. Finally, Ants won the game fair and square, forcing the devil to release the young woman.

Triumphant, Ants returned to the village, and the young woman was reunited with her family. Ants was celebrated as a hero for his bravery and cleverness. From then on, he was known as the man who outsmarted the devil himself!

Mulgi kapsad (Sauerkraut and Barley Stew)

Serves: 4

Introduction:
Mulgi kapsad is a hearty Estonian dish made from sauerkraut and barley.

Ingredients:
300g sauerkraut
200g barley
200g pork (optional)
1 onion, chopped
Salt and pepper to taste
Water or stock

Instructions:
1. In a pot, sauté the onion (and pork if using) until browned.
2. Add the sauerkraut and barley, then cover with water or stock.
3. Simmer for 1 hour, until the barley is tender.
4. Season with salt and pepper before serving.

Tips/Substitutions:
For a vegan version, skip the pork and use vegetable stock.
Serve with rye bread for a traditional touch.

Time to Prep/Cook:
Prep time: 10 minutes
Cook time: 60 minutes

The Birth of Wainamoinen

Finland

Long, long ago, before the world was made, there lived a beautiful maiden named Ilmatar, daughter of the Ether. She floated in the air, for only air and water existed then. One day, she grew tired of always being in the air, so she came down to rest on the water's surface. As she lay there, a fierce storm began, tossing poor Ilmatar through the waves until the wind finally grew still. Worn out, she sank beneath the water, unable to rise again. For seven hundred years, Ilmatar swam, longing to return to the air. At last, she cried out to Ukko, the mighty sky ruler, for help. Just then, a lovely duck flew down, looking for a place to nest. Seeing Ilmatar, the duck landed on her knee and started building its nest. Soon, it laid six golden eggs and one of iron, sitting on them to hatch them.

After three days, the eggs began to heat up, burning Ilmatar's knees. In pain, she moved, causing the nest to slip, and the eggs fell into the ocean, breaking into pieces. But magic happened: the pieces grew huge and formed the sky above and the earth below. The white parts became moonlight, and the yolks became sunlight.

Ilmatar finally raised her head above the water and began creating the land. Where she touched, hills rose, and where she stepped, lakes formed. Where she floated, hidden rocks and reefs appeared, and where she turned her head, deep bays were made.

Once the land was formed, Wainamoinen was born—a wise magician. For seven years, he swam in the ocean, and on the eighth, he stepped onto the land, marking the beginning of his magical adventures.

Lohikeitto (Salmon Soup)

Serves: 4

Introduction:
Lohikeitto is a creamy Finnish salmon soup, often enjoyed during cold winters. It's quick to make and rich in flavour.

Ingredients:
300g salmon fillet, cubed
4 potatoes, peeled and diced
1 carrot, sliced
1 leek, chopped
1 litre fish stock
200ml cream
Fresh dill, for garnish

Instructions:
1. Boil the potatoes, carrots, and leek in the fish stock until tender.
2. Add the salmon and simmer for 5 minutes until cooked.
3. Stir in the cream and season with salt and pepper.
4. Garnish with fresh dill and serve hot.

Tips/Substitutions:
Use coconut milk instead of cream for a dairy-free version.
Serve with a side of rye bread or crispbread.

Time to Prep/Cook:
Prep time: 10 minutes
Cook time: 20 minutes

The Merman

Iceland

Long ago, a farmer from Vogar, famous for his fishing, went out to sea. One day, he felt a heavy pull on his line and reeled in a surprising catch: a merman with a human head and body! The farmer asked the strange creature who he was.

"I am a merman from the sea," he replied, explaining he was adjusting his mother's chimney to the wind when the hook caught him. The merman begged to be set free, but the farmer refused, bringing him to shore instead.

Once on land, the farmer's dog happily greeted him, but the farmer was grumpy and struck the poor animal. This made the merman laugh. Later, while pulling the merman across a field, the farmer tripped over a mound and cursed it, which made the merman laugh again. Finally, when his wife embraced him happily, the merman laughed a third time.

Curious, the farmer asked why he'd laughed three times. The merman promised to explain if the farmer took him back to sea. The farmer agreed, and the merman revealed: he laughed first at the loyal dog, second because the mound was filled with gold, and third because the farmer's wife's embrace was false.

To test the merman's words, the farmer dug up the mound and found a pile of gold coins! Amazed, he returned the merman to the sea.

Soon after, the farmer discovered seven grey cows on the shore. He chased them, bursting a bladder on one's nose, making it tame enough to keep. This cow, a gift from the merman, became famous for her excellent milk and started the beloved breed of grey cows. The farmer prospered and never caught another merman. As for his wife, nothing more is said about her!

Skyr with Berries

Serves: 4

Introduction:
Skyr is a traditional Icelandic dairy product similar to yoghurt, often served with fresh berries for a healthy and simple dessert.

Ingredients:
400g plain skyr
200g mixed berries (blueberries, raspberries, etc.)
2 tbsp honey
1 tsp vanilla extract

Instructions:
1. Mix the skyr with honey and vanilla extract.
2. Divide into bowls and top with fresh berries.
3. Serve immediately for a fresh and healthy dessert.

Tips/Substitutions:
For a vegan option, use plant-based yoghurt and maple syrup instead of honey.
Add a sprinkle of granola for added texture.

Time to Prep/Cook:
Prep time: 5 minutes
Cook time: 0 minutes

The Salmon of Knowledge

Ireland

Long ago, a young boy named Fionn was sent to learn from an old poet named Finnegas, who lived by the River Boyne. One warm spring day, Finnegas told Fionn the tale of the Salmon of Knowledge. Legend had it that this magical salmon ate nuts from a hazel tree that held all the wisdom of the world. The one who ate the salmon, Finnegas explained, would gain all that knowledge. Finnegas had spent many years watching the river, hoping to catch it. One day, as Fionn and Finnegas sat by the river, Finnegas spotted a flash in the water. It was the Salmon of Knowledge! With a quick dive, he caught it and handed it to Fionn, asking him to cook it carefully. But Finnegas made Fionn promise not to taste even a tiny piece. Fionn agreed and set the fish on a hot stone over the fire. While cooking, Fionn noticed that one side of the salmon needed to be turned. As he flipped it over, his thumb brushed against the hot fish, burning him. Instinctively, he put his thumb in his mouth to ease the pain. Just then, he felt a rush of wisdom and power, as if he suddenly understood the world in a way he never had before.
When Finnegas returned, he could sense that something had changed in Fionn. Fionn confessed what had happened, and Finnegas, realising that the salmon's knowledge had been passed to Fionn, told him to eat the rest of the fish. From that day on, whenever Fionn needed wisdom, he would suck his thumb, unlocking the magic of the Salmon of Knowledge. This wisdom would help Fionn become one of Ireland's greatest warriors, famous for his bravery and wit.

Colcannon (Mashed Potatoes with Cabbage)

Serves: 4

Introduction:
Colcannon is a traditional Irish dish of mashed potatoes mixed with cabbage or kale, often enjoyed during Halloween.

Ingredients:
4 large potatoes, peeled and quartered
½ head of cabbage, shredded
50g butter
100ml milk
Salt and pepper to taste

Instructions:
1. Boil the potatoes until tender, then mash with butter and milk.
2. Sauté the cabbage in a little butter until soft.
3. Mix the cabbage into the mashed potatoes and season with salt and pepper.
4. Serve as a side dish or with sausages for a complete meal.

Tips/Substitutions:
Substitute kale for cabbage for a twist on this classic.
For a vegan version, use plant-based butter and milk.

Time to Prep/Cook:
Prep time: 10 minutes
Cook time: 20 minutes

The White Deer

Latvia

Long ago, two brothers wished to become hunters. Their father gave them each a bow, arrows, and a loyal dog. Setting out with excitement, they soon wandered deep into the forest, losing their way. On their journey, they encountered animals they aimed to hunt: two antelopes, two wolves, and two hares. Each animal, in turn, spoke to them, saying, "Don't shoot us. We'll help you in time of need." The brothers agreed, making three animal friends each.

At a crossroads, they decided to part ways and placed knives in an oak tree to signal if either needed help. The elder brother took one path and soon arrived at a grand castle where a young maiden warned him of the mysterious White Deer. Many who pursued it had been turned to stone. The elder brother was determined and chased the White Deer with his animal friends. But a witch tricked him, turning him and his animals to stone. Meanwhile, the younger brother found work in a kingdom, where a dragon threatened the king's three daughters. On three mornings, he secretly defeated the dragon with his animals' help, each time cutting off the dragon's tongues as proof. But a jealous groom took credit, hiding the younger brother's deeds.

When the youngest princess offered him her ring in gratitude, the shepherd returned it to her during the wedding feast, revealing he was the true hero with the dragon tongues. He married the princess, but later remembered his brother. Returning to the oak, he found his brother's knife rusted—a sign of trouble.

The younger brother searched and found his brother, now turned to stone by the witch. With the help of the witch's ashes, he broke the spell, freeing the elder brother, the maiden, and the kingdom's people. They all returned to the castle joyfully, while the White Deer finally ran free through the forest.

Grey Peas with Bacon (Pelēkie zirņi ar speķi)

Serves: 4

Introduction:
Grey peas with bacon is a traditional Latvian dish often served during Christmas.

Ingredients:
200g dried grey peas (or substitute with chickpeas)
100g bacon, diced
1 onion, chopped
Salt and pepper to taste

Instructions:
1. Soak the peas overnight, then boil until tender (about 1 hour).
2. In a frying pan, cook the bacon and onion until crispy.
3. Mix the bacon and onion into the cooked peas and season with salt and pepper.
4. Serve warm as a side dish.

Tips/Substitutions:
For a vegetarian version, skip the bacon and add sautéed mushrooms.
Use canned chickpeas to save time.

Time to Prep/Cook:
Prep time: 10 minutes (plus soaking time)
Cook time: 60 minutes

The Swan Queen

Lithuania

Long ago, an old man and woman lived peacefully in a forest. Each day, when they left to gather sticks, a magical white swan would fly to their house. She would transform into a maid, cook, clean, and prepare everything before leaving, and the couple was grateful but curious about their helper.

One day, the old man hid and saw the swan transform. When she went for water, he burned her wings so she couldn't leave. Heartbroken, she stayed with the couple but missed her family.

One day, the king passed by saw the maid and asked to marry her. She agreed, and soon, they had a son together.

One day, while she was playing with her son in the garden, a flock of swans flew overhead. Leading them was her father, who sang:

"In that garden bright, my daughter I see,
Though she has no wings, yet a swan is she."

Though they offered her wings, she chose to stay with her son. Each day, her family returned, asking her to join them, but she refused. Finally, her true love flew over and sang, but again she declined—for her son's sake.

Sadly, when the king remarried, his new queen, Lauma the Witch, was cruel to the boy. The Swan Queen, now a swan again, secretly visited her son each night, singing him to sleep.

One night, the king saw her. Longing to reunite with his queen, he sought advice from an old man who told him to place tar on the windowsill. When the queen arrived and was caught, the king pulled off her wings, and she returned to human form. Joyful, he banished the wicked queen and held a great feast, inviting all to celebrate. And so, the family was happily reunited, with the Swan Queen finally home for good.

Cold Beet Soup (Šaltibarščiai)

Serves: 4

Introduction:
Šaltibarščiai is a vibrant pink cold beet soup, popular in Lithuania during the summer. It's served with boiled eggs and potatoes.

Ingredients:
4 medium beets, boiled and grated
500ml kefir or buttermilk
1 cucumber, diced
2 hard-boiled eggs, chopped
Fresh dill, for garnish

Instructions:
1. In a bowl, mix the grated beets with kefir or buttermilk.
2. Stir in the diced cucumber and chopped eggs.
3. Garnish with fresh dill and serve cold with boiled potatoes on the side.

Tips/Substitutions:
For a vegan version, use a plant-based yoghurt instead of kefir.
Add a splash of lemon juice for extra tanginess.

Time to Prep/Cook:
Prep time: 15 minutes
Cook time: 0 minutes

The Giant Who Had No Heart in His Body

Norway

Once upon a time, there was a kind King with seven beloved sons. He loved them so much that one always had to be by his side. When the sons grew up, six of them set off to find princesses to marry, while the youngest, Boots, stayed home. The King gave each of the six sons beautiful clothes and splendid horses, and off they went.

After visiting many palaces, the six brothers found six lovely princesses to woo. They were so in love that they forgot to bring a bride back for Boots! As they travelled home, they passed a steep hill where a Giant lived. The Giant saw them and turned them all to stone, including their princesses.

Back at the palace, the King waited anxiously for his sons. When they didn't return, he became very sad. "If only I had not you left," he said to Boots, "I wouldn't want to live!" Boots, determined to find his brothers, asked for permission to set off. The King hesitated, fearing Boots would disappear too, but Boots insisted and finally received his father's blessing.

Boots rode away on an old, broken horse. Soon, he met a starving Raven and gave it some of his food. Then he found a struggling Salmon and helped it back into the water. Next, he encountered a famished Wolf who begged for his horse. Boots agreed, allowing the Wolf to eat his horse, and he climbed onto the Wolf's back.

Together, they reached the Giant's house, where Boots learned from a princess that the Giant had no heart! Boots hid under the bed while the Giant came home. With the princess's help, he discovered that the Giant's heart was hidden far away in a lake.

Boots and the Wolf travelled to the lake, where they found a duck that had the Giant's heart inside an egg. With the help of the Salmon, they squeezed the egg, and the Giant begged for mercy, promising to restore the princes and princesses.

Boots squeezed the egg again, and the Giant burst!

Boots returned home with his brothers and their brides. The King was overjoyed and held a grand feast. Everyone celebrated, and if they aren't still feasting, they are surely dancing in joy!

Fiskekaker (Fish Cakes)

Serves: 4

Introduction:
Fiskekaker are a Norwegian comfort food made from fresh fish, often enjoyed by coastal communities. They are typically served with potatoes, stewed vegetables, or a creamy sauce.

Ingredients:
500g fresh white fish fillets (cod or haddock), chopped
1 small onion, finely chopped
1 egg
2 tbsp potato flour or cornstarch
Salt and pepper to taste
100ml milk
Butter or oil for frying

Instructions:
1. In a food processor, blend the fish fillets until smooth. Add the onion, egg, potato flour, salt, and pepper, then blend again. Gradually add the milk until the mixture is smooth and slightly firm.
2. Shape the mixture into small, flat patties.
3. Heat butter or oil in a frying pan over medium heat. Fry the fish cakes until golden brown and cooked through, about 3-4 minutes per side.
4. Serve with boiled potatoes, steamed vegetables, or a light cream sauce.

Tips/Substitutions:
Alternative Fish: Salmon can be used for a richer flavour.
Dipping Sauce: Serve with a dollop of tartar sauce or lemon aioli for extra flavour.

Time to Prep/Cook:
Prep time: 15 minutes
Cook time: 10 minutes

The Lady of Pintorp

Sweden

Once upon a time, in a place called Pintorp, there lived a mean noblewoman known as the Lady of Pintorp. When her husband passed away, she became the owner of the estate. Instead of being kind, she treated her workers cruelly, locking many innocent people in dungeons and sending vicious dogs after children.

One morning, a farmhand came to work late, and the Lady was furious! She ordered him to chop down the biggest oak tree on the estate and bring it to her castle, or he would lose his home and everything he owned. Feeling hopeless, the farmhand wandered into the woods, where he met an old man. "Don't worry," said the old man. "Chop down the tree, sit on it, and your friends will take it to the castle."

Following the old man's advice, the farmhand quickly cut down the tree, sat on it, and suddenly, it began to move as if pulled by invisible horses. The tree sped towards the castle, leaving a trail of broken fence posts behind!

When the tree reached the castle gate, the Lady of Pintorp saw the farmhand sitting atop the trunk and was furious. Suddenly, the ground shook, and a black coach appeared. A mysterious gentleman dressed in black stepped out and asked the Lady to come with him. Terrified, she begged for more time to prepare, but he only gave her three minutes!

She asked if her chaplain, chambermaid, and valet could join her, and they quickly hopped into the coach. The carriage whisked them away to a grand castle, where the gentleman made her change into a simple dress. He danced with her until she was exhausted, and after each dance, she gave away something valuable, which burned like fire in the hands of her servants.

At the end of the third dance, a trapdoor opened beneath her, and she vanished in smoke and flames. The chaplain, curious about the trapdoor, was blinded in one eye by a spark. The gentleman allowed the remaining servants to return home but warned them not to look back.

However, the chambermaid couldn't resist. As she turned to look, the coach and the road disappeared, leaving them lost in a wild forest. It took them three long years to find their way back to Pintorp, and they would never forget the Lady's terrible fate!

Semla (Swedish Cream Buns)

Serves: 4

Introduction:
Semla is a classic Swedish dessert—soft, cardamom-spiced buns filled with whipped cream and almond paste. This dish is often eaten before Lent.

Ingredients:
250ml milk
25g fresh yeast
500g flour
100g sugar
1 tsp ground cardamom
100g butter, melted
200ml whipped cream
100g almond paste

Instructions:
1. Warm the milk slightly and dissolve the yeast in it.
2. Mix the flour, sugar, and cardamom in a bowl. Add the yeast mixture and melted butter. Knead into a dough and let it rise for 1 hour.
3. Divide the dough into small buns and bake at 180°C for 15 minutes.
4. Once cooled, cut off the top, scoop out a little bread, and fill with almond paste and whipped cream. Replace the top and dust with powdered sugar.

Tips/Substitutions:
Use dairy-free whipped cream for a vegan version.
Add a sprinkle of cinnamon for extra spice.

Time to Prep/Cook:
Prep time: 20 minutes (plus rising)
Cook time: 10 minutes

The Marriage of Robin and Blue Tit

United Kingdom

Once, there was an old grey cat named Poussie Baudrons. One day, she spotted a little Robin Redbreast perched on a bush.

"Where are you going, wee Robin?" she asked.

"I'm off to the king to sing him a song this lovely Yule morning!" chirped Robin.

"Come here, and I'll show you my pretty white neck ring," said Poussie.

"No, no! You scared the little mouse; you won't catch me!" Robin flew away.

Next, he met a hungry hawk.

"Where are you going, wee Robin?" asked the hawk.

"I'm going to sing for the king!" said Robin.

"Come here, and I'll show you a beautiful feather," said the hawk.

"No, no! You snatched up the little finches!" And off he went.

Then he saw crafty Tod Lowrie, the fox.

"Where are you going, wee Robin?" asked Tod.

"I'm off to the king!" Robin replied.

"Come here, and I'll show you my lovely tail," said the fox.

"No, no! You frightened the little lamb!" Robin flew away again.

Finally, he met a little boy by the river.

"Where are you going, wee Robin?" asked the boy.

"I'm going to sing for the king!" Robin said.

"Come here, and I'll give you some treats!" the boy offered.

"No, no! You scared the goldfinch!" And off Robin flew.

At last, he reached the king's castle and sang a beautiful song. The king and queen loved it so much that they decided to give Robin a gift.

"Let's give him the little Blue Tit to be his wife," said the queen.

So wee Robin and the little Blue Tit were married, and they flew home together, happy and full of joy!

Welsh Rarebit

Serves: 4

Introduction:

Welsh Rarebit is a classic British dish from Wales, beloved for its creamy, tangy cheese sauce served over toasted bread. This savoury dish makes a cosy breakfast, brunch, or light dinner.

Ingredients:

200g mature cheddar cheese, grated
2 tbsp unsalted butter
1 tbsp plain flour
2 tbsp ale or milk (for a non-alcoholic version)
1 tbsp Worcestershire sauce
1 tsp English mustard
Salt and black pepper, to taste
4 slices of crusty bread, toasted

Instructions:

1. In a saucepan over medium heat, melt the butter. Add the flour, stirring constantly to form a roux (paste). Cook for 1 minute until smooth.
2. Gradually add the ale or milk, stirring until you have a smooth sauce.
3. Lower the heat and add the grated cheddar, Worcestershire sauce, and mustard. Stir until the cheese is melted and the sauce is smooth. Season with salt and pepper to taste.
4. Toast the slices of bread until golden brown.
5. Place the toast on a baking sheet. Spoon the cheese mixture generously over each slice, covering the edges. Broil for 2-3 minutes, or until the cheese sauce is bubbly and golden.

Tips/Substitutions:

Add a sprinkle of chopped chives or a dash of hot sauce for extra flavour.
A side of mixed greens or a bowl of tomato soup makes this dish a satisfying meal.

Time to Prep/Cook:

Prep time: 10 minutes
Cook time: 10 minutes

Central Europe

Hansel and Gretel

Austria

In a small village by a great forest lived a poor woodcutter, his wife, and their two children, Hansel and Gretel. One year, a terrible famine struck, and the woodcutter could barely feed his family. Worried, he told his wife, "What will we do? We can't feed our children!" His wife had a cruel idea. "Tomorrow, we will take them into the thickest part of the forest, give them some bread, and leave them there. They won't find their way home!" The woodcutter was heartbroken. "I cannot leave my children alone in the woods!"

But his wife insisted until he reluctantly agreed. Hansel and Gretel overheard their mother's plan and were scared. "What will we do?" asked Gretel. "Don't worry," said Hansel. "I'll find a way to help us."

That night, Hansel sneaked out and collected shiny pebbles. The next morning, their mother woke them early and gave them each a piece of bread, telling them not to eat it until lunch. As they walked, Hansel dropped the pebbles behind him.

When they reached the forest, their father lit a fire for them. "Stay here; we will return soon," he said. But when night fell, Hansel and Gretel awoke to find themselves alone. "Don't worry," said Hansel. "We can follow the pebbles home."

The next day, they returned home, and their father was overjoyed, but their mother was furious.

Soon, food was scarce again. Their mother insisted they go deeper into the woods. Hansel crumbled his bread along the way, but this time, the birds ate it all.

After a long day, they were lost and hungry until they found a strange house made of candy. They began to eat it when a wicked witch captured them. She locked Hansel in a cage and forced Gretel to cook for him.

But clever Gretel tricked the witch and pushed her into the oven, saving them both. They found treasure in the witch's house and used it to return home.

Their father was thrilled to see them, and they lived happily ever after!

Wiener Schnitzel (Breaded Veal Cutlet)

Serves: 4

Introduction:
Wiener Schnitzel, Austria's signature dish, is a golden, crispy veal cutlet that symbolises the country's rich culinary heritage.

Ingredients:
4 veal cutlets, pounded thin
2 eggs, beaten
1 cup flour
1 cup breadcrumbs
Salt and pepper to taste
Oil for frying

Instructions:
1. Season veal cutlets with salt and pepper. Dredge each cutlet in flour, dip in beaten eggs, and coat with breadcrumbs.
2. In a skillet, heat oil and fry each cutlet until golden brown, about 3-4 minutes per side. Drain on paper towels.

Tips/Substitutions:
Substitute chicken or pork for a more affordable option.
Serve with lemon wedges and a side of potato salad for an authentic Austrian touch.

Time to Prep/Cook:
Prep time: 10 minutes
Cook time: 10 minutes

The Story of William Tell

Switzerland

Once upon a time in Switzerland, the people were ruled by a cruel tyrant named Gessler, who made their lives very difficult. Among them was a brave man named William Tell, known as the best crossbowman and hunter in the land. One day, he rode into the village of Altdorf with his little son.

Gessler wanted everyone to show their respect, so he placed his cap on a tall pole in the town square and ordered everyone to bow to it. But William Tell stood tall with his arms crossed and laughed at the cap. He refused to bow to Gessler, which made the tyrant very angry. Gessler feared others would follow Tell's example, so he decided to punish him.

To show his power, Gessler came up with a cruel challenge. He forced William Tell's son to stand in the square with an apple on his head, demanding that William shoot the apple with one arrow. William was terrified. "What if I miss? What if I hurt my son?" he pleaded. Gessler threatened that if William failed, his son would be killed. With no choice, William took a deep breath, aimed his arrow, and shot. The arrow struck the apple perfectly!

As William turned away, a second hidden arrow fell from his coat. Gessler shouted, "What is this?" William replied boldly, "That was for you if I had harmed my boy!"

Gessler's anger grew, and he ordered William to prison. But William cleverly escaped and confronted Gessler, defeating the tyrant.

When the townspeople learned of Gessler's defeat, they celebrated William Tell as their hero! They wanted him to be their king, but William refused. He didn't want a lavish life; instead, he returned to his peaceful cottage in the mountains. Thanks to his bravery, the people of Switzerland were finally free!

Rösti (Potato Pancakes)

Serves: 4

Introduction:
Rösti, a Swiss potato pancake, is a simple yet comforting dish enjoyed across the country.

Ingredients:
4 large potatoes, grated
2 tbsp butter
Salt and pepper to taste

Instructions:
1. Squeeze grated potatoes to remove excess moisture. Season with salt and pepper.
2. In a skillet, melt butter and press potatoes into the pan, forming a round pancake. Cook for 10-15 minutes per side until golden brown and crispy.

Tips/Substitutions:
Serve with sour cream or applesauce for extra flavour.
Add onions or cheese for a richer taste.

Time to Prep/Cook:
Prep time: 10 minutes
Cook time: 20-30 minutes

The White Horse of Lochgass

Liechtenstein

On Christmas Eve, in a small village near Vaduz, a notorious horse thief named Jack roamed the streets, looking for his next target. As he walked past the church, he spotted a beautiful white horse tied outside. Its coat shimmered in the moonlight, and Jack's eyes sparkled with greed.

"That horse will be mine!" he thought, sneaking over and untying it. With a swift kick, he hopped onto its back and set off down the road, dreaming of the riches he could get for such a fine creature.

But this was no ordinary horse. As soon as it felt Jack's weight, it reared up and galloped away, tossing him around wildly. Jack pulled at the reins, but the horse was too strong. It raced through the village, over hills, and past fields, running faster than he had ever imagined. Jack clung on for dear life, his heart racing.

"Whoa! Slow down!" he shouted, but the horse wouldn't listen. It leapt and twisted, throwing him off at the top of a steep hill. Jack landed hard, and with a sickening crack, he broke his neck.

As the villagers rushed to the scene, they discovered the truth—the beautiful white horse was actually the Devil in disguise, punishing those who did wrong. After Jack's terrible fate, people began to whisper about the haunted road where the horse had galloped away.

To protect themselves, the villagers decided to build a cross at the spot where Jack fell. They believed it would keep the Devil away and ensure that no other horse thief would suffer the same fate. And from that day on, the road in Vaduz remained peaceful, with no sign of the white horse ever again.

Käsknöpfle (Cheese Dumplings)

Serves: 4

Introduction:
Käsknöpfle, or cheesy dumplings, is Liechtenstein's beloved comfort food, similar to Swiss Alpine dishes.

Ingredients:
300g flour
3 eggs
100ml water
200g grated cheese (Emmental or Gruyère)
1 onion, caramelised
Salt and pepper to taste

Instructions:
1. Mix flour, eggs, and water to form a soft dough. Drop small pieces into boiling water and cook until they float.
2. Drain, layer with cheese in a baking dish, and top with caramelised onions. Bake at 180°C for 10-15 minutes until cheese is melted.

Tips/Substitutions:
Serve with a side of steamed greens or salad.
Add nutmeg for an extra depth of flavour.

Time to Prep/Cook:
Prep time: 15 minutes
Cook time: 20 minutes

Virtue and Fortune in Monte Carlo

Monaco

Once upon a time, in the beautiful Principality of Monaco, the Prince was very sad. His land was dry and barren, and his subjects were poor and struggling. One day, while taking a walk, the Prince stumbled upon a young woman lying still on the ground. She was blindfolded and bound, dressed like the goddesses of ancient Greece. Concerned for her, he had her carried to the most beautiful room in the Palace and cared for.

The next night, the woman awoke and said, "Prince, I am Fortune. I see your troubles, and I want to help you. However, I cannot make your people happy right away. Instead, I will leave you a special talisman. If you learn to use it wisely, it can bring wealth to your land by creating industry." With that, she handed him a simple wooden wheel and vanished.

Days turned into weeks, and the people of Monaco remained poor. Then one bright morning, a curious second-hand dealer arrived in the village. He met with the Prince and, after some negotiation, noticed the wheel that Fortune had left behind. Intrigued, the dealer offered the Prince an annuity that would ensure prosperity for Monaco in exchange for the wheel.

The Prince, desperate to help his people, agreed without hesitation. Unbeknownst to him, the dealer was actually Plutus, the god of wealth. With a flick of his wand, he transformed Monaco. A magnificent palace appeared, surrounded by beautiful gardens, and the marketplace filled with bustling trade and happy faces.

Thanks to the wheel and the magic of Plutus, Fortune had turned her blessings toward Monaco. The land flourished, and prosperity returned to the people, proving that sometimes, a little faith can change everything!

Socca (Chickpea Pancake)

Serves: 4

Introduction:
Socca is a popular street food in Monaco and the French Riviera, made from chickpea flour and olive oil. This crispy pancake is naturally **gluten-free** and can be enjoyed as a snack, appetizer, or light meal.

Ingredients:
250g (1 cup) chickpea flour
500ml (2 cups) water
4 tbsp olive oil (plus more for cooking)
1 tsp salt
Black pepper, to taste
Fresh herbs (such as rosemary or thyme), for garnish

Instructions:
1. Whisk together the chickpea flour, water, 4 tablespoons of olive oil, and salt until smooth. Let the batter rest for at least 30 minutes at room temperature.
2. Preheat your oven to 220°C (425°F). Place a cast-iron skillet in the oven to heat up.
3. Once the oven is hot, carefully remove the skillet or baking sheet and add a tablespoon of olive oil to coat the bottom. Pour in enough batter to cover the bottom of the skillet in a thin layer (about 0.5 cm thick).
4. Return to the oven and bake for 10-15 minutes or until the edges are crispy and the top is lightly browned.
5. Remove from the oven and season with black pepper. Cut into wedges and serve hot, garnished with fresh herbs and a drizzle of olive oil.

Tips/Substitutions:
For extra flavour, mix in finely chopped onions or herbs into the batter before cooking.
Leftovers can be stored in an airtight container in the fridge and reheated in a hot pan.

Time to Prep/Cook:
Prep time: 10 minutes (Resting Time: 30 minutes)
Cook time: 15 minutes

Southern Europe

For The Love of a Dove

Albania

Once upon a time, a lonely princess spent her days knitting in her room. Her mother often urged her to marry, but the princess always said no. One day, a dove flew through her window and brought her joy. The princess exclaimed, "I love you!" The dove replied, "If you truly love me, put a bowl of milk out tomorrow, and you will see my true form."

The next day, the princess poured milk into a bowl. The dove dived in, leaving its feathers behind, and transformed into a handsome young man! They exchanged rings, but he warned, "Never tell anyone my secret and wait three years for my return."

The dove visited every day until one day, the princess could no longer keep the secret from her mother. She blurted, "Leave me alone! I'm wed to a young man!" After that, the dove didn't come back. The princess cried and begged her father for help. He offered her handsome suitors, but she refused. Determined, she asked for iron shoes and walking canes to search for the dove.

Her parents agreed, and she wandered for three years, but no one had seen the dove. When she returned home, her father had painted the palace black in sorrow. Sunburnt and tired, she locked herself in her room. She then asked her father to build a bathhouse where everyone could bathe and tell her stories to relieve her sadness.

One girl in the kingdom heard about the bathhouse. She followed a magical rooster to a house where she discovered the dove's secret. Excited, she rushed to tell the princess her story.

The princess led the girl back to the dove's home. When the twelfth dove appeared, she jumped out and hugged him. He turned back into a man, and they married, living happily ever after!

Tavë Kosi (Baked Lamb with yoghurt)

Serves: 4

Introduction:
This comforting, tangy dish is perfect for family gatherings and celebrations, with its creamy yoghurt sauce contrasting beautifully with the tender lamb and rice base.

Ingredients:
500g (1 lb) lamb shoulder or leg, cut into small pieces
2 tbsp olive oil
Salt and black pepper, to taste
1 cup white rice, rinsed
1 cup plain Greek yoghurt
3 large eggs. 1 tbsp flour
1 ½ cups milk. 2 tbsp butter

Instructions:
1. Preheat the oven to 180°C (350°F). Heat olive oil over medium heat. Add the lamb pieces, salt and pepper, and cook until browned on all sides.
2. Cook the rice according to package instructions until just tender.
3. Beat the eggs. Add the yoghurt, milk, and a pinch of salt, whisking until smooth.
4. Melt the butter. Stir in the flour, whisking until the mixture thickens and becomes smooth. Remove from heat, add the yoghurt mixture.
5. In a baking dish, layer the cooked lamb evenly on the bottom. Sprinkle the cooked rice on top, and pour the yoghurt mixture over the rice and lamb.
6. Bake for 45-50 minutes, or until the top is golden brown and set. Allow to cool slightly before serving.

Tips/Substitutions:
Chicken can be used instead of lamb for a milder flavour.

Time to Prep/Cook:
Preparation Time: 20 minutes
Cook time: 1 hour

The Piper of Ordino

Andorra

Once upon a time, in a lively village, there lived a famous piper named Finn. Finn was known far and wide for his enchanting music, and he was invited to play at a joyful wedding celebration. With his bagpipes slung over his shoulder, he set off, excited to share his tunes.

As he journeyed through the dark forest, Finn suddenly heard rustling in the bushes. To his horror, a pack of hungry wolves emerged, their eyes gleaming and their teeth bared. Thinking quickly, Finn scrambled up a sturdy tree to escape their snapping jaws. As he perched on a branch, he realised he needed to do something to keep the wolves at bay.

With a deep breath, Finn took out his bagpipes and began to play. The sweet melodies echoed through the forest, dancing in the air. The wolves, curious at first, stopped in their tracks, their ears perked up. But as the music continued, something magical happened—the wolves began to sway and howl along with the tunes!

All night long, Finn played his heart out, keeping the wolves mesmerised with his music. They danced and twirled around the base of the tree, entranced by the lovely sounds. Finn was tired, but he knew he had to keep playing to stay safe.

When dawn broke, the villagers, worried about Finn, came searching for him. They heard the distant sound of his pipes and followed the music until they found him, still perched in the tree, surrounded by the sleeping wolves. With great relief, the villagers cheered, "Finn! You're safe!" They helped him down and guided the wolves away.

Finn smiled, knowing that his music had not only saved him but had also brought joy to everyone around. From that day on, he became a legend in the village, celebrated for his bravery and his enchanting tunes.

Escudella (Meat and Vegetable Stew)

Serves: 4

Introduction:
Escudella is a traditional Andorran winter stew with various meats and vegetables.

Ingredients:
500g pork, cubed
100g chorizo sausage, sliced
2 potatoes, diced
2 carrots, chopped
1 cabbage, chopped
Salt and pepper to taste

Instructions:
1. In a large pot, boil pork with salt until tender. Add chorizo, potatoes, carrots, and cabbage.
2. Simmer for 30-40 minutes, seasoning with salt and pepper as needed.

Tips/Substitutions:
Use any favouruite vegetables for added variety.
Serve with crusty bread to soak up the flavours.

Time to Prep/Cook:
Preparation Time: 10 minutes
Cook time: 1 hour

The Dragon's Strength

Bosnia and Herzegovina

Once upon a time, a King had three brave sons. One sunny day, the oldest prince went hunting but never returned. His huntsmen rode back home, confused. "Where's the prince?" the King asked anxiously. "He was chasing a hare near the Old Mill," said the huntsman. "We thought he came home alone."

The next day, the second prince set out to find his brother. He too spotted a hare and followed it, but he vanished as well! Worried, the youngest prince asked to search for them. The King agreed and advised him to go to the Old Mill. The youngest prince, clever and cautious, decided not to chase any hares. Instead, he rode straight to the mill. There, he met an old woman. "Beware, dear boy!" she warned. "A wicked dragon lives here! He lures people with his hare form and traps them in the mill." "What can I do to help you?" the prince asked. "Find out where the dragon's strength lies," she replied, shaking her head sadly. The prince encouraged the old woman to sneak a question to the dragon that night. When the dragon came home, she asked, "Where is your strength hidden?" "Not in my body," he chuckled. "It's in a lake far away, guarded by another dragon!" The next day, the youngest prince disguised himself as a shepherd and went to the lake. He bravely called the dragon out to fight. They wrestled fiercely, but the dragon got tired. "If I could dip my head in water, I could toss you!" he panted. The clever prince replied, "If the Tsar's daughter kisses my forehead, I could throw you even higher!" The princess, who had come to help, rushed forward and kissed him. With newfound strength, the prince tossed the dragon high into the sky, where it burst apart. Out popped a wild boar, a rabbit, a pigeon, and finally, a sparrow, which he captured. "Tell me where my brothers are!" he demanded. The sparrow squawked, "In a dungeon behind the Old Mill! Free them!"

With the dragon defeated, the prince rescued his brothers and the old woman. The King rejoiced, and the youngest prince won the heart of the princess, and they lived happily ever after!

Ćevapi (Grilled Meat Sausages)

Serves: 4

Introduction:
Ćevapi are flavourful grilled sausages popular across the Balkans, traditionally served with pita and onions.

Ingredients:
500g ground beef
200g ground lamb
2 cloves garlic, minced
Salt and pepper to taste

Instructions:
1. In a bowl, combine meats, garlic, salt, and pepper. Shape into small sausage links.
2. Grill on medium-high heat for 5-7 minutes, turning until cooked through. Serve with pita and onions.

Tips/Substitutions:
Use just beef if lamb is unavailable.
Serve with a side of yoghurt for a refreshing dip.

Time to Prep/Cook:
Preparation Time: 10 minutes
Cook time: 10 minutes

Ban Dragonja

Croatia

In southern Istria, Croatia, there lived a friendly giant named Ban Dragonja, who was as big as a mountain! He loved to help the tiny humans living nearby. One sunny day, the villagers asked him to help irrigate their lands by digging rivers. Happy to assist, Ban Dragonja ploughed a long furrow from the lake to the ocean, calling it Dragonja. Then, he created another river and named it Mirna, after his beloved wife.

While digging a third river near the city walls, the giant faced some trouble. The city commander (or his wife, depending on who you ask) scolded him for not digging deep enough. Hurt by their words, Ban Dragonja felt offended and stopped working altogether.

But then, something unexpected happened! The river he had just ploughed began to fill with water, and soon it gushed out, flooding the Pazin valley. The villagers panicked as water rushed in, realising they would drown if the giant didn't return to help them. They called out to him, begging for his assistance.

Hearing their cries, Ban Dragonja felt pity for the frightened villagers. He quickly rushed back to the valley, stomping his massive foot beside the castle. To everyone's surprise, a huge cave opened up beneath him, swallowing all the water!

The villagers cheered and thanked the kind giant for saving them. Ban Dragonja, happy to help once again, promised to keep the rivers flowing and the valley safe.

From that day on, the giant and the villagers lived happily together, knowing they could rely on each other. And so, Ban Dragonja became not just a giant, but a true hero of the land!

Pašticada (Dalmatian Beef Stew)

Serves: 4

Introduction:
Pašticada is a slow-cooked beef dish from the Dalmatian coast, known for its sweet and savoury flavor.

Ingredients:
500g beef, cubed
1 onion, chopped
2 carrots, chopped
100ml red wine
1 tbsp tomato paste
2 bay leaves
Salt and pepper to taste

Instructions:
1. In a pot, brown the beef and onions. Add carrots, tomato paste, red wine, bay leaves, salt, and pepper.
2. Simmer on low heat for 2 hours, stirring occasionally, until the meat is tender.

Tips/Substitutions:
Substitute wine with beef broth if preferred.
Add prunes for a touch of sweetness.

Time to Prep/Cook:
Prep time: 15 minutes
Cook time: 2 hours

Clash of the Titans

Greece

Once upon a time, in the beginning of everything, there was only Chaos, a vast and dark nothingness. But then, out of Chaos, the Earth was born! Mountains rose, the sea flowed, and the sky, called Uranus, filled with the sun, moon, and twinkling stars. Together, Uranus and Earth created mighty children known as the Titans.

However, Uranus was worried that one of his children might take his throne. To protect his power, he trapped them deep inside the Earth! But one brave Titan, Cronus, grew strong and decided to challenge his father. With great courage, he defeated Uranus and became the new leader of the world.

Cronus married Rhea, and they had six children: Hades, Poseidon, Hera, Hestia, and Demeter. Yet, Cronus was just as fearful as his father. He believed that one day one of his own children would take his throne. So, when each child was born, he swallowed them whole!

Rhea, desperate to save her last baby, secretly went to a mountain in Crete to give birth. She named her newborn Zeus and cleverly wrapped a stone in baby clothes. When she presented it to Cronus, he swallowed the stone, thinking it was Zeus!

Zeus was raised by friendly Nymphs who fed him the milk of a goat. When he grew up, Zeus was ready to confront his father. He tricked Cronus into drinking a special potion, which made Cronus spit out all his swallowed children. To everyone's surprise, they emerged fully grown!

With his siblings by his side, Zeus led a great battle called the Titanomachy against the Titans. The war lasted ten years, but the gods triumphed! They cast the defeated Titans into Tartarus, a dark prison far from Earth.

But the adventures weren't over! The gods then fought the Giants in a battle called the Gigantomachy, which they also won. Finally, Zeus became the ruler of the world, and he and the other gods settled on Mount Olympus, living happily ever after.

Spanakopita (Spinach and Feta Pie)

Serves: 4

Introduction:
Spanakopita, a savoury spinach and feta pie wrapped in filo dough, is a popular Greek snack.

Ingredients:
500g spinach, chopped
200g feta cheese, crumbled
1 egg
Filo sheets
Olive oil for brushing

Instructions:
1. Preheat oven to 180°C. Mix spinach, feta, and egg in a bowl.
2. Layer filo sheets in a baking dish, brushing with oil between layers.
3. Spread the spinach mixture, top with more filo, and bake for 30 minutes until golden.

Tips/Substitutions:
Substitute filo with puff pastry if preferred.
Add fresh dill for extra flavour.

Time to Prep/Cook:
Prep time: 15 minutes
Cook time: 30 minutes

The Merchant

Italy

Once upon a time, in a bustling town, there lived a wealthy merchant named Antoniello and his son, Cienzo. One sunny day, while playing by the sea, Cienzo accidentally hit the son of the King of Naples with a stone. Fearing his son would be punished severely, Antoniello panicked and sent Cienzo away with enchanted horses and a magical dog to escape any trouble.

As Cienzo travelled, he came across an old, abandoned house at the foot of a tower. When he tried to find shelter, he heard strange noises inside. Gathering his courage, he went down a ladder into a dark cellar where three ghostly figures cried over a treasure. They gave Cienzo this treasure, telling him to take care of it before vanishing!

Excited, Cienzo continued his journey and soon entered a dark forest where he saw a fairy surrounded by robbers. Without hesitation, he fought bravely and saved her! The grateful fairy invited him to her palace, but Cienzo declined, saying he was in a hurry.

Later, Cienzo arrived at a kingdom in mourning. A dreadful dragon with seven heads was terrorising the land, eating one maiden each day, and the King's daughter, Menechella, was the next target! Cienzo knew he had to help. He bravely confronted the dragon and, after a fierce battle, cut off all seven heads. He sent Menechella home safely, but soon a deceitful countryman claimed credit for Cienzo's heroism!

Realising he had been cheated, Cienzo wrote a letter to Menechella explaining everything and had his enchanted dog deliver it. When the King learned the truth, he crowned Cienzo as the hero instead of the trickster. Cienzo married Menechella, and they celebrated with a grand feast. In the end, Antoniello and his family found favour with the King, proving that sometimes troubles can lead to great fortunes!

Pasta al Pomodoro (Tomato Pasta)

Serves: 4

Introduction:
Pasta al Pomodoro is a classic Italian pasta with a simple, fresh tomato sauce.

Ingredients:
400g spaghetti
500g fresh tomatoes, chopped
2 cloves garlic, minced
Olive oil
Fresh basil
Salt and pepper to taste

Instructions:
1. Cook spaghetti until al dente. In a skillet, sauté garlic in olive oil, then add tomatoes and simmer for 10 minutes.
2. Mix in the pasta, season, and garnish with basil.

Tips/Substitutions:
Add a sprinkle of parmesan for extra richness.
You can add any meat or fish if prefered.
Use cherry tomatoes for a sweeter sauce.

Time to Prep/Cook:
Prep time: 15 minutes
Cook time: 30 minutes

The Tale of the Fisherman's Son

Malta

Once upon a time in Malta, there was a poor fisherman and his son, who lived a simple but happy life by the sea. The boy loved school but eventually decided to leave his studies to help his father with fishing. One day, he caught a gigantic fish and took it to the King as a special gift. The King was impressed and rewarded the boy with gold coins.

The kind-hearted princess, who saw the boy's potential, insisted that he use the money to go back to school. "Study hard," she encouraged, "and you will become wise and knowledgeable!" The boy followed her advice and, over time, he became intelligent and well-read. The princess convinced her father, the King, to allow her to marry him.

At first, the couple was excited, but soon their happiness faded. They often fought, and the princess would call him "just a poor fisherman." Hurt and frustrated, the boy left the palace to live on a distant island, where he became very sad and refused to speak to anyone.

Hearing about her husband's sadness, the princess set off to find him. She found him sitting quietly on the beach, and when she approached, he only wished for her to go away. "I wish you were dead!" he exclaimed, feeling overwhelmed by his heartache.

But in that moment, the boy realised how much he truly cared for her. His heart softened, and he found his voice again. The couple talked about their feelings, apologising for their harsh words and misunderstandings.

With love in their hearts, they returned to the kingdom together. They promised to communicate better and respect each other. From that day on, the fisherman's son and the princess became a happy couple, teaching everyone in Malta the importance of love and respect for those we cherish.

Timpana

Serves: 4

Introduction:
Timpana is a baked macaroni pie with tomato, minced meat, and cheese.

Ingredients:
300g macaroni
200g minced meat
1 onion, chopped
200ml tomato sauce
100g grated cheese
1 egg, beaten
Salt and pepper to taste

Instructions:
1. Preheat oven to 180°C. Cook macaroni until al dente. In a pan, cook onion and meat, then add tomato sauce, salt, and pepper.
2. Mix with pasta, add egg, and transfer to a baking dish. Top with cheese and bake for 20-30 minutes until golden.

Tips/Substitutions:
Use gluten-free pasta if needed.
Add diced bell peppers for extra flavour.

Time to Prep/Cook:
Prep time: 10 minutes
Cook time: 30 minutes

The Legend of Black Lake

Montenegro

Once upon a time, in a small village in Montenegro called Brezna, an old lady named Mala shared a special legend about Saint Sava. "Good afternoon, Mala! How are you today?" a curious child asked.

"Just like an old lady should be—old and tired," Mala replied with a smile. "Can you tell me the story of Saint Sava?" the child eagerly asked.

"Of course! Saint Sava, may mercy be upon him, was celebrated everywhere, especially in my school. We would sing songs about him on his special day. He was from Bosnia and Herzegovina, and one day, while riding his horse, he arrived in Brezna to warm the cold village. The Joković family invited him to stay the night but played a trick on him. In the morning, they claimed he had stolen from them, showing him a rooster hidden in his bags. Furious, Saint Sava cursed the village, deciding it would always be cold there. "Was it really that cold back then?" the child asked.

"Oh yes! People struggled to stay warm," Mala explained. "When he left Brezna, he went to a place now known as Black Lake. There was a monastery there, and when Saint Sava opened his bags, he found only old bread for him and his students, while everyone else had delicious food. Angry, he made a cross with his cane and cursed the monastery, causing it to sink into the lake! "What about the horse?" the child wondered. "Ah, Jabućilo! He was a magical horse who belonged to a duke. Jabućilo still comes out of the lake sometimes, but he doesn't want any mares nearby!" Mala chuckled.

"Does he come out often?" the child asked.

"No one knows when, but he enjoys visiting other horses now and then," Mala said with a twinkle in her eye.

"Thank you for the story, Mala! It's so interesting!" the child exclaimed. "You're welcome, my dear! Montenegro has many tales full of wisdom and magic!" And so, the legend of Saint Sava continued to be told, sharing the rich traditions of Montenegro with each new generation.

Kačamak
(Cornmeal Porridge with Cheese and Potatoes)

Serves: 4

Introduction:
Kačamak is a hearty Montenegrin dish made with cornmeal, cheese, and potatoes.

Ingredients:
300g cornmeal
2 potatoes, diced
100g cheese (such as feta or kajmak)
Salt to taste

Instructions:
1. Boil potatoes until soft, then mash them in the pot.
2. Gradually stir in cornmeal, adding water as needed to reach a thick, porridge-like consistency.
3. Add cheese and mix until melted and creamy. Serve warm.

Tips/Substitutions:
Serve with a dollop of sour cream or extra cheese on top.
Use gluten-free cornmeal if needed.

Time to Prep/Cook:
Prep time: 10 minutes
Cook time: 30 minutes

Justice Never Dies

North Macedonia

Once in autumn, a kind boy found an eagle with hurt wings. Feeling sorry for it, he took the eagle home and cared for it all winter long. As spring arrived, the eagle's wings grew new feathers.

"You can fly now! Go back to your friends," the boy said, smiling.

The eagle flapped its wings happily. "You've been so good to me! What can I do for you?" it asked.

"Why would an eagle help me?" the boy replied, puzzled.

"Take one of my feathers," said the eagle. "If you ever need me, beat the feather between two stones, and I'll come to help."

The eagle flew away, and the boy set out to explore the world. While walking by a river, he spotted a man deep in thought. Behind the man lurked a hungry wolf!

"Look out! There's a wolf behind you!" the boy shouted. The man jumped into the river, and the wolf ran off.

Later, the boy found a big fish stranded on the bank. He gently pushed it back into the water. "Thank you! What can I do for you?" the fish asked.

"Nothing, I just helped," replied the boy.

"Please, take one of my scales. If you need help, beat the scale between two stones, and I'll come to you."

As the boy continued his journey, he met the man he had saved from the wolf. The man smiled and said, "I want to reward you for saving my life."

"What are you?" the boy asked, curious.

"I am the devil!" the man replied. The boy was scared.

"Don't worry," said the devil. "Take three hairs from my head to the king's daughter. She is looking for someone to hide from her for three days. If you succeed, you can marry her. Burn my hairs, and I'll help you."

The boy agreed and began his adventure. He knew he could call on the eagle and the fish for help.

Tavče Gravče (Baked Beans)

Serves: 4

Introduction:
Tavče Gravče, a baked bean dish, is a North Macedonian favourite often served at gatherings.

Ingredients:
300g white beans, soaked overnight
1 onion, chopped
2 cloves garlic, minced
1 bell pepper, chopped
1 tbsp paprika
Salt and pepper to taste

Instructions:
1. Boil the beans until tender, then drain. In a skillet, sauté onions, garlic, and bell pepper. Add paprika, salt, and pepper.
2. Combine beans with the sautéed mixture in a baking dish, and bake at 180°C for 30 minutes.

Tips/Substitutions:
Serve with warm freshly baked bread bread and fresh herbs on top.
Add smoked sausage, bacon or porcini mushrooms for added depth.

Time to Prep/Cook:
Prep time: 10 minutes
Cook time: 1 hour

St. Anthony's Godchild

Portugal

Once upon a time, there was a man with so many children that he struggled to find godfathers for them all. When his last child was born—a sweet, dark-eyed girl—he decided to ask the first person he met on the street. Luckily, he ran into the kind St. Anthony. "Will you be the godfather to my daughter?" he asked. St. Anthony smiled and agreed, naming the baby Antonia. "Train her well," he said, "and when she turns thirteen, I will return to help her." Years flew by, and soon Antonia was thirteen. The father worried that St. Anthony had forgotten his promise. But one day, St. Anthony appeared, looking at Antonia with delight. "Dress like your brothers; I'm taking you to the king's court," he said. Antonia changed into her brother's clothes and became known as Anthony, serving as a page to the king. The king had a sister who became fond of Anthony, but when he didn't return her feelings, she got angry and plotted against him. She told the king that Anthony claimed he could separate all the chaff from wheat in a single night. The king, curious, told Anthony to prove it.

Worried but remembering St. Anthony's support, Anthony called for his godfather's help. By morning, the wheat was perfectly clean! The king loved Anthony even more, but the sister remained jealous and plotted again. She claimed that Anthony boasted he could steal a purse of gold from the king of the Moors. The king ordered Anthony to do it. With St. Anthony's guidance, he succeeded, sneaking in and taking the purse without waking the king of the Moors. Next, the sister demanded that Anthony capture the king of the Moors himself. Nervous, Anthony once again sought St. Anthony's help. He quietly climbed into the palace, rolled the king in his bedclothes, and tossed him out the window into a boat.

When Anthony returned with the king as his captive, the king was amazed. "You're worthy of any honour. You shall marry my sister!"

"I can't marry her," said Anthony. "I am actually Antonia!"

"In that case," the king replied with a grin, "I'll marry you myself!"

Pastéis de Nata (Custard Tarts)

Serves: 4

Introduction:
Pastéis de Nata are creamy Portuguese custard tarts with a caramelised top, originating in Lisbon's monasteries.

Ingredients:
1 sheet puff pastry
200ml milk
3 egg yolks
100g sugar
1 tbsp flour
Vanilla extract

Instructions:
1. Preheat oven to 200°C. Roll and cut puff pastry into circles, pressing into a muffin tin.
2. Whisk milk, sugar, egg yolks, flour, and vanilla in a saucepan. Heat until thickened, then pour into pastry cups.
3. Bake for 15-20 minutes until tops are golden.

Tips/Substitutions:
Dust with cinnamon or powdered sugar before serving.
Use coconut milk for a dairy-free option.

Time to Prep/Cook:
Prep time: 15 minutes
Cook time: 20 minutes

The Legend of Saint Peter's Mother

San Marino

Once upon a time, there was a legend about Saint Peter's mother. She was known to be greedy and cold-hearted, giving only one leaf of celery to the poor throughout her life. This tiny gift was given by accident when she dropped it, but even that wasn't enough to earn her kindness points!

Despite this, her son Peter, a saint, tried to convince God to let her into Heaven because of that one leaf. However, when she began boasting about how she deserved to go to Heaven just because her son was a saint and that she was better than everyone else, God decided she was not fit for Heaven after all. So, she was sent back to Hell, her pride proving to be her downfall.

In contrast, the story of Madonna's House had a much happier ending. It began like the tale of Hansel and Gretel, where children were sent into the woods and lost their way home. But instead of a witch's cottage, they stumbled upon a lovely little house belonging to the Virgin Mary. Inside, they found warmth, love, and safety.

They grew up there, happy and cherished, under the watchful eye of Mary, who cared for them like a mother. Another story that reminded me of this was about a poor girl who chose to buy a doll instead of bread. Her sisters scolded her for being foolish, but when she woke up the next morning, she found gold pieces hidden in the doll's nappy! This surprise showed that sometimes, unexpected kindness and generosity can come from the smallest acts.

Torta Tre Monti (Three Mountains Cake)

Serves: 4

Introduction:
Torta Tre Monti, a layered chocolate-hazelnut wafer cake, represents the three peaks of San Marino's Mount Titano.

Ingredients:
4 wafer sheets
200g chocolate or hazelnut spread
100g dark chocolate, melted

Instructions:
1. Spread chocolate or hazelnut spread between wafer layers. Stack them to form a cake.
2. Pour melted chocolate over the cake and let it set before slicing.

Tips/Substitutions:
Use gluten-free wafers if needed.
Garnish with crushed hazelnuts for extra crunch.

Time to Prep/Cook:
Prep time: 10 minutes
Cook time: None (assembly only)

How to Choose a Wife

Serbia

Once upon a time, there was a man who found himself in a puzzling situation. His friends wanted him to marry one of three women: a young maid, a widow, or a divorced woman. Each was good-looking and kind, but he couldn't decide who to choose! So, he decided to seek advice from an old man in his village.

The wise old man listened carefully and said, "I can't give you an answer, but you should ask the Allwise King Solomon. He will know what is best. Go to him and come back to tell me what he advises."

The man set off to King Solomon's court. When he arrived, the guards asked what he needed, and he replied, "I wish to see the Allwise." One of the guards led him to a child playing in the courtyard on a stick.

"Is that the Allwise?" the man wondered. But he approached the child anyway, curious to hear what he had to say.

King Solomon, stood on his stick and asked, "What brings you here?" The man shared his dilemma, explaining the three women he was considering.

The child thought for a moment and replied, "When you marry a maid, she will look up to you. If you marry a widow, she may think she knows better. But if you choose a divorced woman—beware of my horse!" With that, the child gently tapped the man's feet with his stick and resumed riding.

The man left, feeling foolish for asking a child for advice. When he returned to the old man, he angrily recounted what happened. The old man chuckled and explained, "The child's words were wise! A maid will respect you; a widow may challenge you; but a divorced woman could scold you like she did her first husband. Choose wisely, my son!"

Pileći Paprikaš (Serbian Chicken Paprikash)

Serves: 4

Introduction:

Pileći Paprikaš is a flavourful Serbian chicken stew featuring tender chicken cooked in a rich paprika-based sauce.

Ingredients:

4 chicken thighs or drumsticks
1 large onion, finely chopped
1 red bell pepper, chopped
2 cloves garlic, minced
2 tbsp paprika (sweet or smoked, as preferred)
1 tsp tomato paste
salt and pepper, to taste
1 cup chicken broth
1 cup sour cream (or yoghurt, for a lighter option)
1 tbsp vegetable oil

Instructions:

1. In a large pot, heat the vegetable oil over medium heat. Add the chicken thighs and cook until browned on all sides, about 4-5 minutes per side. Remove the chicken and set aside.
2. Add the chopped onion, bell pepper, and garlic. Sauté the onions and the peppers.
3. Stir in the paprika and tomato paste.
4. Pour in the chicken broth and return the chicken to the pot. Season with salt and pepper. Cover and simmer for 30-40 minutes, until the chicken is tender and cooked through. Stir in the sour cream.

Tips/Substitutions:

Small diced potatoes can be added for extra heartiness.
ileći Paprikaš pairs wonderfully with rice.

Time to Prep/Cook:

Prep time: 10 minutes
Cook time: 45 minutes

The Tale Of Goldhorn

Slovenia

Once upon a time, in the enchanting Valley of Triglav, there lived beautiful nymphs known as the White Women. They guarded their magical home fiercely, and anyone who dared to approach was chased away by stone avalanches triggered by the White Goats that lived on the mountain ridges, led by a magnificent creature called Goldhorn. His golden horns held the key to great treasures hidden on Bogatin Mountain, but if he was ever hurt, a special flower called the Triglav flower would grow from his blood. If Goldhorn ate even a single leaf of this flower, he would heal instantly. The only mortal who could reach the highest peaks was the Trenta Hunter, the son of a beautiful widow, who was said to have been blessed by the White Women at his birth. He often brought stunning flowers from the mountains to his sweetheart, the landlord's daughter, known for her beauty and kindness. One Sunday, as winter melted into spring, Italian merchants visited the tavern where the Hunter's sweetheart worked. A wealthy young man tried to win her heart with golden rings and pearl necklaces, charming her with music and dance. When the Hunter arrived to ask her for a dance, her eyes told him she preferred the merchant. Hurt, he left. The Green Hunter, known for leading young men into trouble, persuaded the Trenta Hunter to capture Goldhorn and claim his treasures. That very night, they climbed the mountains in search of the magical creature. The Hunter managed to wound Goldhorn, who retreated to a narrow ledge, where beautiful Triglav flowers grew. Suddenly, Goldhorn recovered, his golden horns shining brighter than ever. In his excitement, the Trenta Hunter lost his footing and fell into the abyss. Meanwhile, the landlord's daughter regretted how she treated him and waited for his return. Sadly, as the snow melted, the river brought his lifeless body home. Goldhorn, angry from losing his home, destroyed the blooming pastures, leaving only a rocky landscape behind. The White Women vanished forever, and the valley was never the same again.

Potica (Nut Roll)

Serves: 4

Introduction:
Potica, a rolled pastry filled with nuts, is a traditional Slovenian dessert enjoyed at festive gatherings.

Ingredients:
200g walnuts, ground
200g flour
50g sugar
1 egg
50ml milk
Butter for greasing

Instructions:
1. Make a dough with flour, sugar, egg, and milk. Roll it out and spread ground walnuts over the surface.
2. Roll up the dough, place in a greased pan, and bake at 180°C for 30-40 minutes.

Tips/Substitutions:
Use almonds instead of walnuts for variety.
Dust with powdered sugar for a decorative finish.

Time to Prep/Cook:
Prep time: 20 minutes
Cook time: 40 minutes

The Legend of the Spider

Spain

Once upon a time, in a grand kingdom, there lived a spoiled Princess named Uru. She was her father's favourite and was surrounded by luxurious gifts, beautiful clothes, and endless parties. Her father tried hard to teach her how to be a wise and responsible ruler, but Princess Uru paid little attention. Instead of studying, she spent her days focused on fashion and travelling, often ignoring her lessons and the needs of others.

Tragically, her father passed away unexpectedly, and Princess Uru became Queen at a very young age. At first, she responded well to her father's advisors and listened to her people, but that didn't last long. As days turned into weeks, Queen Uru grew bored with her responsibilities. She began to ignore her duties and complain about how tedious ruling could be. Anyone who dared to disagree with her or suggest that she take her role seriously was punished or thrown into prison.

As Queen Uru became more tyrannical, the people of the kingdom began to fear her. One day, in a fit of anger, she was about to strike an innocent person when something strange happened—her arm froze in mid-air! It is said that an Incan Goddess appeared before her, disappointed by Uru's selfishness. As punishment, the Goddess stripped the Queen of her beauty, strength, and riches, transforming her into a small, hairy spider.

Queen Uru was horrified! By the time she realised what had happened, it was too late. She could no longer complain about her duties, and instead, she was forced to weave intricate spiderwebs for the rest of her life, catching tiny insects as her only source of food. From that day on, the once-spoiled princess learned the hard way that true beauty and strength come from kindness and caring for others.

Tortilla Española
(Potato Omelette)

Serves: 4

Introduction:
Tortilla Española, a hearty Spanish potato omelette, is enjoyed as a tapa or main dish throughout Spain.

Ingredients:
4 potatoes, thinly sliced
1 onion, sliced
4 eggs
Olive oil
Salt to taste

Instructions:
1. In a skillet, cook potatoes and onions in olive oil until tender. Beat eggs and pour over, cooking until set.
2. Flip onto a plate, then slide back into the skillet to cook the other side.

Tips/Substitutions:
Serve warm or at room temperature with a side salad.
Add bell peppers or chorizo for extra flavour.

Time to Prep/Cook:
Prep time: 10 minutes
Cook time: 20 minutes

Eastern Europe

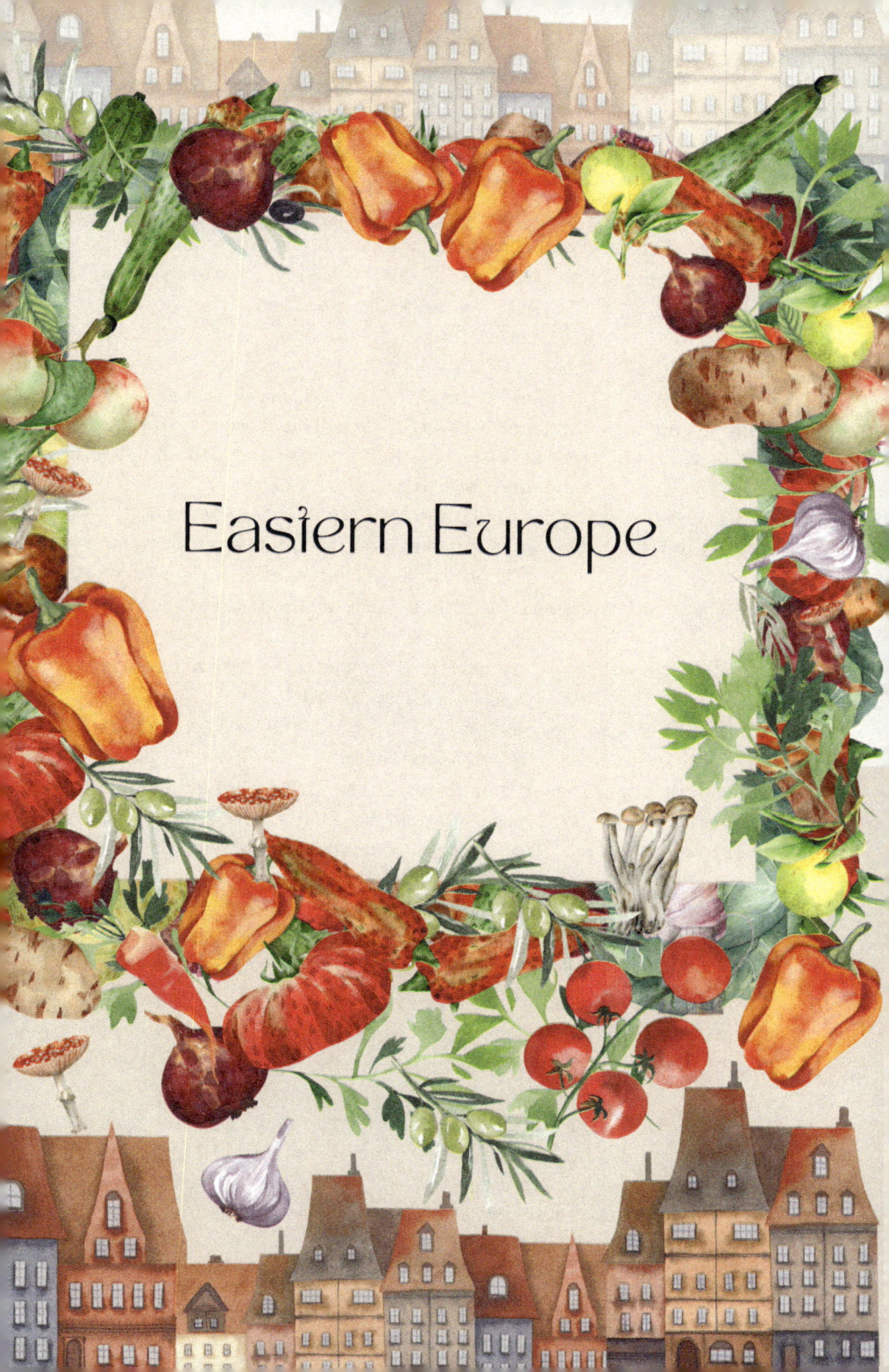

The Mower and the Wolf

Belarus

One sunny day, a mower was hard at work in the meadow. When he got tired, he sat down under a bush to rest. He took out his small bag and began to chew on some bread. Just then, a hungry wolf emerged from the woods. Spotting the mower, the wolf approached and asked, "What are you eating, man?"

"Bread," the mower replied.

"Is it delicious?" asked the wolf.

"Yes, it is," said the mower.

"Could I have a taste?" the wolf requested.

"Here you are," the mower said, sharing some of his bread. The wolf enjoyed it and asked, "I wish I could eat bread every day, but how can I get it?"

The mower replied, "I'll teach you how to get bread." He explained that the wolf needed to plough the soil, sow rye, and then wait all winter.

"Oh," sighed the wolf, "that's such a long wait! Will I have bread?"

"No, you won't!" the mower interrupted, explaining more about making bread.

"Isn't there an easier way?" asked the wolf, sounding disappointed.

"Look at the flock of grazing sheep over there," the mower suggested. The wolf quickly ran to the field and approached the largest ram. "Ram, ram! I'm going to eat you!" the wolf declared.

"Okay," said the ram. "But I don't want to suffer long. You'd better stand by the hill and open your mouth wide. I'll jump in."

"Thanks for the advice!" replied the wolf. So, they set up the plan. The ram charged up the hill and butted the wolf on the head with all his strength! The wolf's eyes rolled back, and he fell to the ground.

When the wolf came to his senses, he shook his head, wondering if he had eaten anything. Meanwhile, the mower finished his work and chuckled, saying, "No, you haven't eaten the ram, but you sure tried the easiest way to get food!"

Draniki (Potato Pancakes)

Serves: 4

Introduction:
Draniki are crispy Belarusian potato pancakes, a beloved comfort food.

Ingredients:
6 large potatoes, grated
1 onion, finely chopped
2 eggs
3 tbsp flour
Salt and pepper to taste
Oil for frying

Instructions:
1. Squeeze out excess liquid from the grated potatoes.
2. Mix the potatoes, onion, eggs, flour, salt, and pepper in a bowl.
3. Heat oil in a frying pan. Scoop small amounts of the mixture into the pan, flattening them into pancakes.
4. Fry for 3-4 minutes on each side until golden brown. Serve with sour cream or applesauce.

Tips/Substitutions:
For a gluten-free option, replace flour with cornstarch.
Add a bit of grated carrot for extra colour and sweetness.

Time to Prep/Cook:
Prep time: 10 minutes
Cook time: 10 minutes

The Witty Petar

Bulgaria

Once Witty Petar went to the market without any money. He saw a soup vendor selling delicious soup. As he didn't have money with him, Witty Petar took a piece of bread out of his pocket and held it in the tasty-smelling steam coming out of the soup pot. After a while, the bread was well-flavoured, and Witty Petar ate it. Seeing this, the vendor asked Witty Petar to pay for the food.
"But I just held my bread over the steam, I won't pay" said Witty Petar.
"If you won't pay, then you deserve to be beaten with a stick" the vendor said.
"No problem. But if I flavoured the bread using your steam, then you should beat only my shadow" said Witty Petar
Everyone at the market started laughing at the greedy vendor.

***

One day the Witty Petar met his long time rival Nastradin Hodja. Knowing that Petar was funny, Nastradin Hodja asked him to tell him one of his jokes.
"No problem. Just wait for me to go home and get my sack of jokes" said Witty Petar.
Nastradin Hodja stayed there for hours before he finally understood that he had already taken part in the joke.

Banitsa (Cheese Pastry)

Serves: 4

Introduction:
Banitsa is a savoury Bulgarian pastry filled with cheese, often enjoyed for breakfast or as a comfort food.

Ingredients:
500g filo pastry
400g feta cheese, crumbled
3 eggs
100ml milk
50g butter, melted

Instructions:
1. Preheat oven to 180°C.
2. In a bowl, mix the crumbled feta, eggs, and milk.
3. Layer a sheet of filo pastry in a greased baking dish, brush with melted butter, and add a spoonful of the cheese mixture. Repeat until all layers are complete.
4. Bake for 30 minutes until golden and crispy.

Tips/Substitutions:
You can add spinach for a spinach and cheese version.
For a dairy-free option, use vegan cheese.

Time to Prep/Cook:
Prep time: 15 minutes
Cook time: 30 minutes

The Long-Desired Child

Czech Republic

In a small hut at the edge of a village, a poor man and his wife lived together. The man worked as a labourer, while the woman spun yarn to sell. Despite their struggles, they often wished for a child, saying, "If only we had a little one!" Their neighbours warned, "Be thankful you don't! You barely have enough to eat!" But the couple replied, "Once we are satisfied, we would always have some food for our child." One day, while digging in the forest, the man stumbled upon a root that looked like a little child. Excited, he took it home and said to his wife, "Look! It's our child, an Otesanek! You can raise him!"

The woman wrapped the root in swaddling clothes and sang to it. Suddenly, the root kicked and cried, "Mother, I'm hungry!" Delighted, she rushed to prepare food. After devouring everything she offered, Otesanek cried out, "Mother, I want more to eat!" The woman, surprised, borrowed a loaf of bread from a neighbour. As she left the room, Otesanek quickly climbed off the bed and gobbled up the bread. When she returned and saw him, she gasped, "Otesanek! You ate the loaf?" "Yes, and now I'll eat you!" he replied, swallowing her whole before she could react. When the man came home, Otesanek shouted, "Father, I'm hungry!" The father was terrified to see his son so large. Otesanek grinned, "I've eaten your wife, and now it's your turn!" In an instant, the man was swallowed too. Otesanek was still hungry, so he wandered into the village. He encountered a girl with a wheelbarrow of clover and devoured her. Then he met a peasant with a cart of hay, a swineherd with pigs, a shepherd with sheep, and an old woman tending cabbages. He swallowed them all until the wise old woman struck him with her mattock, splitting him in half.

Out jumped everyone Otesanek had eaten, and they all returned home, happy to be free. From that day on, the couple never wished for a child again!

Svíčková (Beef Sirloin with Cream Sauce)

Serves: 4

Introduction:
Svíčková is a traditional Czech dish made with beef in a creamy vegetable sauce.

Ingredients:
500g beef sirloin
2 carrots, chopped
1 onion, chopped
1 celery root, chopped
200ml cream
100ml beef broth
2 tbsp flour
2 tbsp oil

Instructions:
1. Brown the beef in oil and set aside. In the same pot, sauté the carrots, onion, and celery root.
2. Add the beef broth and return the beef to the pot. Simmer for 1 hour.
3. Remove the beef, blend the vegetables into a sauce, and stir in the cream and flour.
4. Slice the beef and serve with the creamy sauce and bread dumplings.

Tips/Substitutions:
You can use vegetable broth for a vegetarian sauce version served over tofu.
Serve with cranberry sauce for a traditional touch.

Time to Prep/Cook:
Prep time: 15 minutes
Cook time: 1 hour 15 minutes

The Gold Bread

Hungary

Once upon a time, in a little village, lived a widow and her beautiful daughter, Marienka. While the mother was humble and kind, Marienka was filled with pride. Many suitors came to win her heart, but she turned them all away, saying, "None of you are good enough for me!"

One night, while Marienka slept, her mother prayed for her happiness. Marienka laughed in her sleep, and the next morning, she shared her dream of a nobleman in a copper coach putting a sparkling ring on her finger.

That same day, a handsome farmer asked for her hand, but Marienka dismissed him, saying, "Even if you came in a copper coach, I wouldn't marry you!"

The next night, she laughed again, dreaming of a nobleman in a silver coach. Soon after, another young lord proposed, but again she refused, saying, "Even if you came in a silver coach, I wouldn't marry you!"

On the third night, Marienka laughed loudly again. She dreamt of a nobleman arriving in a golden coach, and the next day, three splendid coaches arrived: one copper, one silver, and one golden. A handsome nobleman asked for Marienka's hand. Delighted, she accepted, believing her dreams had come true.

But her mother worried and asked, "What bread do you offer my daughter?" The nobleman replied, "She can choose from copper, silver, or gold bread."

Marienka soon found herself in a magical castle with the King of the Mines. At a feast, she realised she couldn't eat any of the food!

Three times a year, Marienka returned to the village dressed in rags, begging for scraps. When she received a little bread, she felt happier than in her palace, learning that true happiness comes from kindness, not pride.

Goulash (Beef Stew)

Serves: 4

Introduction:
Goulash is a famous Hungarian stew made with beef, paprika, and vegetables.

Ingredients:
500g beef, cubed
2 onions, chopped
2 potatoes, diced
2 carrots, chopped
1 red pepper, chopped
2 tbsp paprika
1 tsp caraway seeds
1 tbsp tomato paste
750ml beef broth
Salt and pepper to taste

Instructions:
1. Sauté the onions in a pot until soft, then add the paprika and caraway seeds.
2. Add the beef and cook until browned.
3. Stir in the tomato paste, broth, potatoes, carrots, and red pepper. Simmer for 1.5 hours until tender.
4. Season with salt and pepper. Serve hot with crusty bread.

Tips/Substitutions:
For a vegan version, substitute beef with mushrooms and beans.
Add a dollop of sour cream to each serving for extra richness.

Time to Prep/Cook:
Prep time: 15 minutes
Cook time: 1 hour 30 minutes

The Pot of Gold

Moldova

Once upon a time, a hardworking man had three strong sons. Sadly, they were lazy and preferred to sit in the shade or go fishing instead of helping their father. Neighbours often asked them, "Why don't you help your father?" They shrugged and replied, "He takes care of everything!"

As the years passed, the father aged and could no longer work. The garden grew wild, and the fields were overrun with weeds. No matter how much he urged them to help, his sons continued to lounge around.

One day, the father fell ill and called his sons to his bedside. "My end is near," he said. "How will you live without me?"

The sons were worried and asked for his final advice. "Your mother and I saved a pot of gold over the years. I buried it near the house, but I forgot where. Find it, and you'll be rich!" he said, before taking his last breath.

Grief-stricken, the brothers decided to search for the pot of gold. They grabbed their spades and dug around the hut, but found nothing.

"Let's dig deeper!" suggested the youngest brother. They dug and dug until the eldest brother felt something hard.

Excited, he called his brothers over. They all worked together but uncovered only a large stone.

Disappointed, they decided to throw the stone away. After that, they dug up the entire garden, but still found no treasure.

Finally, the eldest brother said, "Since we've dug up the garden, let's plant grapevines!" His brothers agreed, and they carefully tended to the vines.

Before long, their hard work paid off with a bountiful harvest of juicy grapes. They kept some for themselves and sold the rest for a good profit.

The eldest brother smiled and said, "We discovered the real treasure our father spoke of—working together brought us happiness and success!"

Mămăligă (Cornmeal Porridge)

Serves: 4

Introduction:
Mămăligă is a traditional Moldovan cornmeal porridge, often served as a side dish. It can be served alongside Goulash.

Ingredients:
1 litre water
250g cornmeal
1 tsp salt
50g butter

Instructions:
1. Bring the water to a boil in a pot and add the salt.
2. Gradually stir in the cornmeal, stirring constantly to prevent lumps.
3. Cook for 15 minutes, stirring often, until thickened.
4. Stir in the butter and serve hot, either as a side or with cheese.

Tips/Substitutions:
For a creamier version, stir in some cheese at the end.
Serve with a dollop of sour cream or as a base for stews.

Time to Prep/Cook:
Prep time: 5 minutes
Cook time: 15 minutes

Twardowski

Poland

Once upon a time, a nobleman named Twardowski wanted to be wiser than everyone else. More than anything, he feared death and wanted to find a magical potion to live forever. He learned how to summon demons from an old book and left Cracow at midnight to practice his magic in Podgorze.

Soon, a demon appeared, and Twardowski made a pact, promising his soul if the demon could catch him in Rome. Twardowski ordered the demon to gather all the silver in Poland and bury it, which is how the famous silver mines of Olkusz were created. He commanded the demon to bring a large rock to Piaskowa Skala, where it stands today as Hawk's Rock. Twardowski could do anything he wished, from flying without wings to travelling faster than a horse.

One day, he fell in love with a young lady who challenged him to guess the creature she kept in a bottle. Disguised as a beggar, he guessed correctly, and they married. However, Twardowski often teased her by sending servants to break her pottery, enjoying her angry reactions.

Eventually, Twardowski grew tired of his magical games and went into the forest to think. Suddenly, the demon appeared and demanded he go to Rome. Angry, Twardowski used a spell to drive the demon away, but the demon struck him with a pine tree, leaving him with a broken leg and earning him the nickname "Gameleg."

As time passed, the demon grew impatient and disguised himself as a servant, luring Twardowski to a tavern named Rome. Realising the trap, Twardowski quickly picked up a baby to protect himself. The demon couldn't take him while he held the innocent child.

The demon, frustrated, whisked Twardowski high into the sky. As he flew, he sang a hymn he wrote as a child. Miraculously, the hymn brought him to a stop in mid-air, and the demon disappeared.

Now, Twardowski remains suspended in the sky, waiting for judgment day, and on clear nights, people still point to a dark spot in the sky, wondering if it's Twardowski himself.

Pierogi (Dumplings)

Serves: 4

Introduction:
Pierogi are iconic Polish dumplings, stuffed with a variety of fillings like potatoes, cheese, or sauerkraut.

Ingredients:
250g flour
1 egg
100ml water
400g potatoes, mashed
100g cottage cheese
Salt and pepper to taste
Butter for frying

Instructions:
1. Mix the flour, egg, and water into a dough. Roll out and cut into circles.
2. Combine the mashed potatoes and cheese. Place a spoonful of filling onto each circle and fold into half-moons, sealing the edges.
3. Boil the pierogi for 3 minutes, then fry in butter until golden.

Tips/Substitutions:
Add sautéed onions for extra flavour in the filling.
For a sweet version, fill with fruit and dust with powdered sugar.

Time to Prep/Cook:
Prep time: 20 minutes
Cook time: 10 minutes

The Enchanted Pig

Romania

Once upon a time, there was a King with three daughters. One day, he had to go to battle. Before he left, he gathered his girls and said, "I must go away. Take care of yourselves, be good, and stay away from the room at the back of the palace. It's forbidden."

The daughters promised to be good and waved goodbye as their father left. At first, they kept busy by sewing, reading, and playing in the garden. But soon, curiosity about the forbidden room grew too strong.

The eldest daughter said, "Why can't we explore that room? We've seen everything else!" The youngest protested, "But Father warned us!" However, the other two persuaded her to join them, and they unlocked the door.

Inside, they found a table with a big, open book. Excited, the eldest read aloud, "The eldest daughter will marry a prince from the East." The second daughter giggled, "I can't wait to marry my prince!" But when the youngest read, "The youngest daughter will marry a pig from the North," she gasped in horror.

Heartbroken, the youngest Princess grew sad and pale, while her sisters married their princes. One day, a pig came to the palace, claiming he wanted to marry the youngest Princess. The King had no choice but to agree.

On their journey home, the pig rolled in mud and asked her to kiss him. Though she felt grossed out, she remembered her father's words and did it. At night, she discovered the pig transformed into a handsome man!

But one night, she accidentally broke a magic thread that kept him human. "Now, you must search for me!" he said sadly before disappearing.

Determined, the Princess travelled far and wide, facing many challenges. She met the Moon and the Sun, who helped her learn that her husband was hidden deep in a thick wood. Using chicken bones she had saved, she built a ladder to reach his home.

Finally, she found him! Their love had broken the spell, and they lived happily ever after, together once more.

Ciorbă de burtă (Beef Tripe Soup)

Serves: 4

Introduction:
Ciorbă de burtă is a tangy Romanian soup made with beef tripe, perfect for cold days and hangover.

Ingredients:
500g beef tripe
1 onion, chopped
2 carrots, chopped
4 cloves garlic, minced
1 litre beef broth
100ml sour cream
2 tbsp vinegar
Salt and pepper to taste

Instructions:
1. Boil the tripe in water for 1 hour, then drain and set aside.
2. In a pot, sauté the onions, carrots, and garlic. Add the broth and tripe. Simmer for another hour.
3. Stir in the vinegar and sour cream. Season with salt and pepper and serve hot.

Tips/Substitutions:
Use chicken or mushrooms for a less adventurous, more family-friendly version.
Serve with crusty bread for dipping.

Time to Prep/Cook:
Prep time: 15 minutes
Cook time: 2 hours

Baba Yaga

Russia

Once upon a time, there was a man and his daughter. After the girl's mother passed away, the father married again, but the new stepmother didn't like the girl. She mistreated her and plotted to get rid of her. One day, the wicked stepmother told the girl to visit her aunt and ask for a needle and thread to sew a blouse. Little did the girl know, her "aunt" was Baba Yaga, a bony old witch!

Before going, the clever girl visited her real aunt for advice. "You'll face many challenges," her aunt warned. "A birch tree will try to hit you; tie it with a ribbon. The gates will creak; oil the hinges. The dogs may chase you; throw them fresh rolls. And if you see a cat, give it ham." Thanking her aunt, the girl set off for Baba Yaga's hut.

When she arrived, Baba Yaga was spinning. "Good day, Auntie," the girl said. "Mother sent me for a needle and thread." Baba Yaga agreed but told her to weave first. While the girl worked, Baba Yaga ordered her servant to prepare a bath, planning to eat the girl for breakfast! Panicking, the girl begged the servant, "Please don't burn the wood! Use a sieve to carry water instead." The servant, grateful for a kerchief the girl gave her, agreed.

As Baba Yaga peeked in, the girl whispered to the cat, asking for help. "Take this comb and towel to escape!" the cat said. "When Baba Yaga chases you, throw down the towel to make a river. If she crosses it, throw the comb to create a forest!"

The girl ran. She threw fresh rolls to the dogs, oiled the gates, and tied the birch tree. Meanwhile, the cat tangled the weaving. Baba Yaga rushed in, furious to find the girl gone! She scolded her helpers, who replied, "We helped her because she treated us kindly!"

From that day on, the girl lived happily, free from the wicked stepmother's grasp.

Blini (Buckwheat Pancakes)

Serves: 4

Introduction:
Blini are traditional Russian buckwheat pancakes, often served with sour cream, jam or caviar.

Ingredients:
200g buckwheat flour
200ml milk
2 eggs
1 tbsp sugar
1 tsp baking powder
Oil for frying

Instructions:
1. Mix the flour, eggs, milk, sugar, and baking powder into a smooth batter.
2. Heat a little oil in a frying pan and pour in small amounts of batter to form pancakes.
3. Fry for 2-3 minutes on each side until golden. Serve with sour cream, jam, or honey.

Tips/Substitutions:
For a gluten-free version, use 100% buckwheat flour.
Add a pinch of cinnamon for extra warmth.

Time to Prep/Cook:
Prep time: 10 minutes
Cook time: 10 minutes

The Story of Three Wicked Yezinkas

Slovakia

Once upon a time, there was a poor boy named Yanechek. His parents were gone, and he had to find work on his own. After wandering a long way, he came upon a small house near the woods. An old man sat on the doorstep, blind, for he had no eyes.

The old man's goats bleated nearby, hungry to graze. "You poor things," the old man said, "I'd take you to the pasture if I could see."

"Let me take them, grandfather," Yanechek offered. Grateful, the old man warned him, "But don't go to the hill in the woods—the Yezinkas may catch you!" Yanechek knew Yezinkas were wicked witches disguised as lovely maidens, and if you fell asleep near them, they would take your eyes!

The first two days, Yanechek stayed away from the hill, but on the third day, he thought, "There's better grass there. I'm not afraid of the Yezinkas." Before setting out, he cut three blackberry switches and tucked them in his hat.

While Yanechek sat watching the goats, a beautiful maiden in white appeared and offered him an apple. But he knew she was a Yezinka and refused. Next, a second maiden appeared with a rose, and he refused her too. Finally, a third maiden appeared with a golden comb. Just as she tried to comb his hair, Yanechek took a switch and struck her hand. She couldn't move, for Yezinkas are helpless if touched by blackberry switches!

Yanechek tied her hands, and as her sisters rushed to help, he struck them too. He then brought his master to the Yezinkas, demanding they return his eyes. Twice, they tried to trick him with animal eyes, but Yanechek tossed the tricksters into the river! The third sister finally gave the old man his eyes back, and he could see once more. From then on, Yanechek and the old man lived happily, never troubled by the Yezinkas again!

Bryndzové Halušky (Potato Dumplings with Sheep Cheese)

Serves: 4

Introduction:
Bryndzové Halušky are soft potato dumplings served with salty sheep cheese, a national dish of Slovakia.

Ingredients:
500g potatoes, grated
150g flour
1 egg
200g sheep cheese (Bryndza)
100g bacon, diced
Salt to taste

Instructions:
1. Grate the potatoes and mix with flour, egg, and salt to form a dough.
2. Drop small pieces of the dough into boiling water and cook until they float to the surface.
3. Drain the dumplings and mix with sheep cheese and bacon.

Tips/Substitutions:
Use feta cheese as a substitute for Bryndza.
For a vegetarian version, omit the bacon and use fried onions instead.

Time to Prep/Cook:
Prep time: 15 minutes
Cook time: 10 minutes

How the Dog Found Himself a Master

Ukraine

Long ago, dogs were wild and free like wolves, with no masters. But one dog grew tired of being alone, always searching for food and fearing stronger animals. So he set out to find a powerful master to protect him.

He first met a big, fierce wolf. "Where are you going, Dog?" asked the Wolf. "I'm looking for a master. Will you be mine?" "Why not?" said the Wolf. So, they travelled together.

As they walked, the Wolf suddenly froze, sniffed the air, and darted into the bushes. The Dog was puzzled. "What's wrong, Wolf?" he asked. "There's a Bear ahead," said the Wolf, trembling. "He could hurt both of us!" Realising the Bear was stronger, the Dog left the Wolf and asked the Bear to be his master.

"Come with me," the Bear said, "and I'll kill a cow for us to eat."

They set off but were stopped by a loud, frightening noise. The cows were running wildly, mooing in panic. The Bear peeked out, then quickly hid.

"It's the Lion!" whispered the Bear, scared. "He's the mightiest animal."

The Dog thought, if the Lion is the strongest, he should be my master! He left the Bear and approached the Lion, who agreed to be his master. Life with the Lion was peaceful, and no one dared harm the Dog.

One day, while walking together, the Lion suddenly stopped, roared, and began backing away. "What's wrong, Lion?" asked the Dog.

"I smell a man approaching. He's stronger than I am!" said the Lion, nervously retreating. Hearing this, the Dog decided to find the man and ask him to be his master.

The Dog joined the man and became his faithful companion. This happened long, long ago, but ever since then, the dog has been loyal to people, serving them with all his heart. And that is why dogs are known as man's best friend to this very day!

Borscht (Beetroot Soup)

Serves: 4

Introduction:
Borscht is a vibrant beetroot soup loved across Ukraine, served hot or cold with sour cream.

Ingredients:
4 beetroots, peeled and grated
1 onion, chopped
2 carrots, chopped
2 potatoes, diced
1 cabbage, shredded
1 litre vegetable broth
2 tbsp vinegar
200ml sour cream
Salt and pepper to taste

Instructions:
1. Sauté the onion and carrots in a pot, then add the broth, beetroots, potatoes, and cabbage.
2. Simmer for 30 minutes until the vegetables are tender.
3. Stir in the vinegar and season with salt and pepper. Serve with a dollop of sour cream.

Tips/Substitutions:
For a vegan version, skip the sour cream or use a dairy-free substitute.
Add a dash of dill for extra flavour.

Time to Prep/Cook:
Prep time: 10 minutes
Cook time: 30 minutes

Western Europe

The Magic Cap

Belgium

Once, a poor farmer named Jan was known for being simple-minded, and people often tricked him. One day, Jan's wife asked him to take their calf to market and sell it for a fair price. So Jan set off, leading the calf.

As he walked, three mischievous students saw Jan and decided to play a joke. The first student approached him and said, "How much are you selling your goat for?"

"A goat?" said Jan, confused. "This is a calf!"

The student chuckled, "Looks like a goat to me! Maybe your wife was joking." And he left, laughing.

Next, another student came along and told Jan, "That's clearly a goat!" Jan felt uneasy. Then, a third student appeared, also calling the calf a goat. By now, Jan was so puzzled that he handed over the calf, saying, "If it's a goat, I don't want it!" The students laughed, taking the calf.

When Jan told his wife, she was furious but also clever. She hatched a plan and set up meals at three inns for the next market day, leaving instructions with each innkeeper. She told Jan what to do, and he followed her advice exactly.

The next week, Jan met the students again and invited them to join him for food and drinks. At each inn, Jan twirled his cap, saying, "Everything is paid for, right?" The servers, following his wife's instructions, agreed.

The students were amazed. Finally, they asked Jan about his "magic cap," which he claimed could make anything free. They begged to buy it. Jan played along and sold it for a hefty sum of 500 francs!

Later, the students tried using the cap to get a free meal with friends. But when they twirled it, nothing happened, and the innkeeper demanded payment! Realising they'd been tricked, the students had to pay up, while Jan and his clever wife counted the coins back home, laughing at their cleverness. And so, Jan was tricked no more!

Stoofvlees (Belgian Beef Stew with Beer)

Serves: 4

Introduction:
Stoofvlees is a beloved Belgian stew made with beef and Belgian beer, known for its rich, caramelised flavour.

Ingredients:
500g stewing beef, cubed
2 large onions, chopped
500ml Belgian beer (or dark ale)
2 tbsp flour
2 tbsp mustard
2 tbsp brown sugar
2 bay leaves
2 tbsp butter
Salt and pepper to taste

Instructions:
1. In a pot, melt the butter and brown the beef. Remove beef and set aside.
2. In the same pot, sauté the onions until soft, then sprinkle flour and stir.
3. Return the beef to the pot, add beer, mustard, sugar, bay leaves, salt, and pepper.
4. Cover and simmer for 2 hours, stirring occasionally, until the meat is tender. Serve with fries or crusty bread.

Tips/Substitutions:
For a non-alcoholic version, use beef broth with a splash of vinegar for depth.
Add carrots or mushrooms for extra heartiness.

Time to Prep/Cook:
Prep time: 15 minutes
Cook time: 2 hours

The Wild Boar

France

One day, Ourson was in the forest chopping wood, waiting for his friend Violette to bring him lunch. Violette was eager to see him and took a shortcut through the forest with a basket of treats. As she walked, she suddenly heard heavy footsteps—an enormous wild boar came crashing through the trees, looking furious!

Terrified, Violette climbed a tree just in time as the boar charged at her. It rammed the tree repeatedly, but she clung tightly to the branches. The wild boar eventually tired, lying at the tree's base, but stayed close, eyeing her angrily.

Violette called for help, hoping Ourson would hear. Ourson, wondering why Violette hadn't arrived, took a shortcut through the forest and soon heard her cries. Running toward her voice, he saw the wild boar and Violette perched in the tree. Summoning his courage, Ourson ran at the boar with his axe. The boar attacked him fiercely, but Ourson bravely dodged and fought.

Suddenly, a bird appeared singing a funny tune, distracting the boar. It looked up, confused, then slowly backed away and finally left. Ourson, exhausted but unharmed, climbed up to help Violette down. She was relieved and grateful to see her friend safe.

As they prepared to head home, Violette was too weak to walk, having lost her lunch basket. Just then, a magical bundle appeared at their feet with food and drink! They ate happily and rested, thankful for their safety.

It was getting dark, so they decided to stay in the forest for the night. Ourson made a cosy bed for Violette and lay nearby to protect her. In the morning, they found their way back home safely before their mother woke up, keeping their adventure a secret. Only their trusted friend Passerose heard about the wild boar and their brave escape. The two friends returned to their happy lives, grateful for each other and the magic that kept them safe.

Quiche Lorraine

Serves: 4

Introduction:
Quiche Lorraine is a classic French tart filled with cream, cheese, and bacon.

Ingredients:
1 pie crust (or shortcrust pastry)
200g bacon, chopped
200ml heavy cream
3 eggs
100g grated Gruyère cheese
Salt and pepper to taste

Instructions:
1. Preheat oven to 180°C. Line a pie dish with the crust.
2. Fry the bacon until crispy. In a bowl, whisk the eggs, cream, cheese, salt, and pepper.
3. Sprinkle the bacon over the crust, pour the egg mixture on top, and bake for 30-35 minutes until golden.

Tips/Substitutions:
Substitute bacon with sautéed vegetables for a vegetarian version.
Add nutmeg for a hint of warmth.

Time to Prep/Cook:
Prep time: 10 minutes
Cook time: 30 minutes

Ashenputtel

Germany

Once, a kind girl lost her mother, who, before she passed away, told her, "Be good and pious, and I'll look down on you from heaven." The girl missed her mum dearly, and every day she visited her mother's grave to cry and pray.
After some time, her father remarried a woman with two daughters. But they weren't nice to the girl; they made her do all the chores, and soon she was called Ashenputtel because she was always covered in ashes. She wore only old clothes while her stepsisters dressed in fine outfits.
One day, her father went to a fair and brought Ashenputtel a hazel twig. She planted it by her mother's grave, watered it with her tears, and a beautiful tree grew there. A white bird in the tree granted any wish she made.
When the king invited all the young women to a festival so his son could find a bride, Ashenputtel wished to go. Her stepmother scattered lentils in the ashes, saying she could only go if she picked them all up. Ashenputtel called to the birds, and they helped her! But her stepmother still wouldn't let her go.
Heartbroken, Ashenputtel went to the hazel tree, and the bird dropped a gown of gold and shoes of silver for her. At the festival, the prince danced with Ashenputtel all night, not recognising her under her splendid dress. She left before he could follow her home, running back to her cinders and her plain clothes.
On the last night, the prince secretly spread pitch on the steps. When Ashenputtel fled, her golden shoe got stuck! The next day, the prince searched for the girl whose foot fit the tiny shoe. The stepsisters tried to squeeze into it, but only Ashenputtel's foot fit perfectly. The prince knew she was the mysterious girl he'd fallen for and made her his bride.
Ashenputtel forgave her family, but they were punished for their cruelty, while she and the prince lived happily ever after.

Sauerbraten (German Pot Roast)

Serves: 4

Introduction:
Sauerbraten is Germany's famous pot roast, marinated in vinegar and spices for a tangy, deep flavour.

Ingredients:
500g beef roast
250ml vinegar
500ml beef broth
1 onion, sliced
2 bay leaves
5 peppercorns
2 tbsp flour
2 tbsp oil
Salt and pepper to taste

Instructions:
1. Marinate the beef in vinegar, onion, bay leaves, and peppercorns for 2-3 days in the refrigerator.
2. Remove the beef from the marinade and pat dry. Brown it in oil, then add the marinade and broth.
3. Cover and simmer for 2 hours, then thicken the sauce with flour. Serve with mashed potatoes or red cabbage.

Tips/Substitutions:
Use apple cider vinegar for a milder tang.
For faster preparation, marinate for just 24 hours.

Time to Prep/Cook:
Prep time: 10 minutes (plus marinating)
Cook time: 2 hours

The Legend of Beautiful Melusina

Luxembourg

Long ago, Count Siegfried, a brave knight, became lost in a misty, deep valley. There, he found the ruins of an ancient castle on a cliff and heard a beautiful song. He followed the sound and found a mysterious maiden, Melusina, a water spirit, singing near the castle ruins. Siegfried fell in love with her instantly.

The two began meeting, and soon, Melusina agreed to marry Siegfried on one condition: he could never look for her on Saturdays. Siegfried promised, and in time, he traded his land for the rocky cliffs where Melusina lived. The mysterious figure of Satan then offered to build Siegfried a grand castle overnight if Siegfried would surrender his soul after thirty years. Eager to be with Melusina, Siegfried accepted. By morning, a magnificent castle stood tall on the cliffs, and the two were married.

For years, they lived happily, and Melusina gave birth to seven children. Every Saturday, she disappeared, always locking her door. Siegfried kept his promise, never questioning her. But one day, curious friends whispered doubts into Siegfried's mind, and his curiosity got the better of him.

On a Saturday, Siegfried peeked through Melusina's keyhole and saw her bathing, combing her long hair—but instead of legs, she had a mermaid's tail! Shocked, he cried out. Hearing him, Melusina gasped and vanished into the cliffs, never to return.

But the legend says that Melusina still appears every seven years, searching for someone brave enough to break her spell. Once, a soldier tried to save her, but he failed, and now, the people of Luxembourg hear her haunting cry when danger approaches.

Until she's freed, Melusina is said to work on a magical shirt, sewing one stitch every seven years. Only when the shirt is complete will her spirit finally be free. And so, the people of Luxembourg remember the mysterious Melusina, who watches over their city from the cliffs.

Judd mat Gaardebounen (Smoked Pork with Broad Beans)

Serves: 4

Introduction:
Judd mat Gaardebounen is Luxembourg's national dish featuring smoked pork neck with beans, a hearty meal with a rustic charm.

Ingredients:
500g smoked pork neck or ham
1 onion, chopped
2 carrots, chopped
500g broad beans (or fava beans)
Salt and pepper to taste

Instructions:
1. Boil the pork neck in a pot with onions and carrots for 1.5 hours.
2. Add the broad beans and cook for an additional 15 minutes.
3. Slice the pork and serve with beans, seasoning with salt and pepper to taste.

Tips/Substitutions:
Substitute broad beans with green beans for a lighter option.
Serve with mustard or crusty bread for extra flavour.

Time to Prep/Cook:
Prep time: 10 minutes
Cook time: 1 hour 45 minutes

The Mouldy Penny

Netherlands

Long ago, when fairies and magical creatures were everywhere, the Dutch had a saying: "Gold makes a woman penny-white." Back then, pennies were made of silver and shined so brightly that they could light up anyone's face. Before they used money, Dutch people traded things like salt for furs or fish for tools. Life was simple and their needs were few.

Over time, merchants from the South brought fancy goods, like mirrors, jewellery, and clothes. People began to want these items, so they learned to use money, made of shiny coins. But people quickly found that money could bring both happiness and trouble. Some saved their coins and used them wisely; others spent them quickly, and still others hid their coins away, letting them gather dust without helping anyone.

The fairies, known as kabouters, thought this was funny. They decided to play tricks on people, especially those who hoarded money selfishly. One day, two kabouters discussed three brothers who each used their first silver penny differently.

The first brother, a miser, hid his penny, but the kabouter stole it and hid it in an old boat. The second brother was kind; he used his money to help others, and he saved it to build an orphan house. The third brother, however, spent all his money foolishly and left his family poor.

Years later, when a canal was dug in the village, workers found an ancient boat. Inside was a moldy silver penny—the one the kabouter had hidden so long ago. The penny had turned black, covered in dust and wax.

The villagers remembered the lesson: money, when shared, can do great things, like helping orphans or supporting families.

Stamppot (Mashed Potatoes with Kale)

Serves: 4

Introduction:
Stamppot is a hearty Dutch dish of mashed potatoes mixed with kale or other greens, often served with sausage.

Ingredients:
1kg potatoes, peeled and chopped
300g kale, chopped
100ml milk
2 tbsp butter
4 smoked sausages
Salt and pepper to taste

Instructions:
1. Boil the pork neck in a pot with onions and carrots for 1.5 hours.
2. Add the broad beans and cook for an additional 15 minutes.
3. Slice the pork and serve with beans, seasoning with salt and pepper to taste.

Tips/Substitutions:
For a vegan option, use plant-based milk and sausage.
Add a spoonful of mustard to the mash for a traditional Dutch twist.

Time to Prep/Cook:
Prep time: 10 minutes
Cook time: 20 minutes